HIDDEN BRUISES IN HOLY PLACES

A Victim's Voice

Unmasking Narcissistic Religious Abuse.
Exposing the Pain. Healing the Hurting.

Michele Armstrong

Carpenter's Son Publishing

Published by Carpenter's Son Publishing, Franklin, TN.

Published in association with Larry Carpenter of
Christian Book Services, LLC
www.christianbookservices.com

Edited by Bob Irvin

Cover and Interior Design by Suzanne Lawing

Cover illustration by Michelle Wilson

Printed in the United States of America

ISBN 978-1-952025-40-2

True Greatness

A dedication to the love of my life who passed from this life on February 11, 2021, during the publishing process of this book: In this world where power, prestige, fame, and fortune configure the definition of greatness, I know different because of a man named Jeff Armstrong. A gentle, quiet man of steel, who could have built skyscrapers and repaired rocket ships with his skilled hands and incredibly intelligent mind, Jeff exemplified greatness at nearly every moment I was privileged to know him. He spent his spare time in simple ways such as browsing hardware, tractor supply, and home improvement stores, further developing his craft. The world should have known him. Jeff was a rare treasure and the world became the loser when he passed from this earth. Jeff embodied the definition of greatness. I expressed on a social media post that the universe shifted a little the day Jeff passed away, and it did. Or at least I know mine did, and I will never be the same.

After living the nightmare of abuse for thirty years in my former marriage to a minister, I was blessed to be the recipient of complete healing and deepest joy through the vessel of a man name Jeff Armstrong. When I met Jeff at work while I was a leasing agent for Nickel Plate Properties, he barely spoke a word to me. Many times when he entered the office, he would simply nod my direction and keep walking. On a mission to fulfill the millions of tasks before him, he could not be bothered with pleasantries or chitchat. Intrigued as I witnessed his work ethic, stability, integrity, and uncompromising pursuit of excellence, I knew I wanted to know him more. Eventually, I gained the honor of becoming his wife.

Both of us having been broken from the past onslaughts of Satan trying to destroy us, we created a life together neither of us ever dreamed possible, full of gratitude for the gift of each other. The love spilled over in our conversations and into our daily lives. We were soul mates, deliriously in love and extraordinarily grateful. Even though we came at situations from different planets, we were perfect for each other. He kept my balloon tethered just enough to let me fly without completely soaring aimlessly into space, while I opened his mind to new wonders he had never experienced before. Our life together was perfect, and Jeff unashamedly expressed to people that God had brought us together. My beautiful Jeff would take my breath away when he walked into the room or when he looked into my eyes, and his eyes would well up with tears as he told me he loved me and how beautiful I was to him. His presence gave me safety, security, comfort, love, and peace. When the world was going crazy, Jeff was always there, sure and steady, dispelling my every fear, ensuring me through one touch of his massive, strong hand that the world could never hurt me again as long as he was there.

Through the years of his adult life before I met him, Jeff had allowed Satan to reign in his life and made choices that nearly destroyed him. Having lived a wild and riotous life trying to find his value and happiness at the bottom of the bottle or through other false comforts, those deceitful comforts lost their glimmer—and Jeff had lost nearly all hope. He swirled in a cesspool of despair, hopelessness, and misery. That's when Jesus stormed in. In his hopeless state, Jeff cried out for God to come into his life. From that moment, his life drastically changed, and everyone who knew him witnessed the transformation. People were constantly telling me of the change they saw in Jeff. He had come to the end of himself and trusted in the saving power of Jesus. Not long after that moment, I showed up. One of the first activities we did together was go buy him a Bible. He stood in the store in tears expressing his gratitude for this most precious gift of the Word of God in print. I will never forget that day. And that is the way we lived our lives together—with Jesus at the helm guiding us through every moment of every day.

Jeff would want everyone reading this to know about the saving power of Jesus, the Son of the living God. He would want you to know that your life, too, can be radically changed from hopelessness and despair to a life of peace and joy. And that your value is beyond compare as you trust in the One who died for you. Jeff's life since knowing Jesus was not without trials, but it was also never again without hope. As he passed peacefully from this life in his last few moments on earth, the transition to glory was peaceful and full of hope. He would want the same for everyone else. Jeff would say today, "If you don't know Jesus, please begin to at this moment. You will never regret the choice to do so." He would want his life to be a legacy of the saving power of the Son of God, Jesus the Christ.

During his last moments on earth, I anointed Jeff's body with oil in hopes that Jeff would be healed from the atrocity his heart had committed against his body. The Scripture teaches there is healing in this act. And although I didn't get the result I desired, it was as though I had the honor of anointing him for burial. Like the woman who anointed Jesus' feet and knew there was no greater thing she could do for him to express her love and devotion, I too felt the honor of caressing the strong but broken body of the greatest man I have ever been privileged to know—a final act of service I was honored to perform for the love of my life. Satan didn't win. The sacrifice of praise and prayer has been profoundly answered. Jeff has received his healing. Praise the Lord!

And now as I embark on this journey of figuring out the life and plans God has for me, just as I did nine years ago when I found myself alone and afraid, I do not fear this time. Because I believe that God will lead me into a life I treasure just as he did when he led me to my Jeff. And though it seems now that my future life will pale in comparison as far as having the companionship and overflowing love I had with my Jeff, I know my future will be shaped by a loving God. My Jeff would want me to follow whatever path on which God leads me, and I will do that. And it will be full of greatness—not because of me, but because of the truly great men who have helped shape me: my Jesus and my Jeff. Whoever I am able to touch with the love and healing power of Jesus, I am convinced it is an extension of the love and healing Jesus afforded me through a simple but truly great man named Jeff Armstrong.

Jeff, I will love you and honor you until the day I die. And then I will come to be with you forever where we will stroll over Heaven together. That day will not come soon enough, my love. But in the meantime, I will raise a hallelujah at the top of my lungs, and you will be part of it. I adore you, my precious love. You saved me. My love for you is boundless, and I am so blessed to have lived seven years and eighty days of my life with you. I wouldn't trade one of them to save me from an ounce of the pain of losing you. You are my angel.

See you soon.

Hallelujah.

Michele

Dedication

To my beautiful Debbie. You taught me to climb trees, braid my hair, and chase rainbows. You saw the warning signs and tried to save me, didn't you? I know you didn't live long enough on earth to see it, but I am victorious. I know you're in Heaven rejoicing, my friend, my sister, my angel. I love you. See you soon.

And to Katie Beth. A million galaxies cannot contain my love for you. You are gifted in the spiritual realm, my beautiful Kingdom Princess. Be a warrior. Defeat the darkness. Lead people to the light. Change the world. You are spectacular.

Acknowledgments

My Jeff. You saved me. My love for you is boundless, and I am so blessed to be doing life with you. You are my angel.

John and Seth. This book is your story too. But most importantly, it is testament to our shared victory. You both are the heart that beats within me. We made it through together. I would do it all again simply for the blessing of being your mother.

Jenny and Ellie. My "daughters" given to me by God, Heaven-sent as wives for my sons. I couldn't love you more if you were my own flesh and blood. You have surpassed what I could have dreamed daughters-in-law could be.

My Daddy and Mama. You were always a safe place to land. Your cherished teachings created a foundation that strengthened me in the darkest hours. I love you with all my heart. I will always be immensely grateful for you both. Thank you for everything.

Brenda, Beci, Rena, Kelley, Polly, English, Eva, and Sharon. The truest friends on the planet. Words fail to express what you mean to me and how each of you have uniquely embellished my life. You are more than friends; you are sisters.

Linda Walsh. Thank you from the bottom of my heart for the countless hours and many months of editing my original draft, providing me a manuscript I could proudly submit for publishing. What an indescribable gift! You are a treasure.

Michelle Wilson and Ellie Bamburg. My deepest gratitude for your incredible insight and advice on the cover design. Michelle, your graphic design skills are truly a gift. You both helped me create a cover beyond what I imagined. You brought my vision to reality. Thank you.

Saray Taylor-Roman. Thank you for the gift of supplying me with the photographs of my dreams. I have never felt more beautiful. God has bestowed special favor upon your talent and skill. You are truly an artist.

Warren Kyle. I thank you deeply for helping fund the publishing of this book. Any way in which God may choose to use it, you will always be a part of that. God bless you, my dear friend.

Judy Graham and Jessica Richard. I can never thank you enough for the glorious days of rest and renewal at Hidden Haven Cabin. Some gifts are priceless, and I deeply appreciate your amazing generosity. You will never know what it has meant. I love you like family.

Chrys Howard. If not for your recommendation of my amazing publisher and new friend, Larry Carpenter, I'm not sure I would have a completed book. God used you in mighty ways. Thank you, my beautiful friend.

Contents

Foreword

Evil can disguise itself in many ways. One of these is the spiritual deception of others.

For years, our sweet friend and sister in the Lord, Michele Armstrong, endured this type of evil. She and her sons were controlled, brainwashed, and abused by a man who professed to be called to ministry by God.

It is sad that many times such a thing goes on right under our noses, in our churches, in our pulpits! Even in an open church that shares each other's burdens and holds people accountable, we do not know what goes on in certain narcissistic-dominated homes.

One in four women suffer in silence in our pews, in isolation and abandonment. The ones who love them too often sit by helplessly knowing any wrong move could bring trauma to those "under the spell." The victims don't know they are victims. Their abusers have veiled their eyes with assault. Michele and her children were no different. She was always trying to be "a better wife" and the kids were always trying to "please their father." It was to no avail.

When you read this book with open eyes and an open heart (a heart that will break), let God direct your next move. Some of you may recognize what's happening to those you know and love. Some may see themselves in Michele's story. Some of you will not want to finish the book, but please, I implore you to read all of it. Everyone will need to act on what you've learned.

We must first believe their story.

We must offer a safe place.

We must support and encourage.

We must help the victims find healing.

We must rid our pulpits, our leadership, and our churches of these abusers. There's no excuse when we turn a blind eye to this tragedy.

Michele is a strong, courageous, brave woman. She allowed God to direct her out of the trauma and into a healing relationship with Him. God has healed her and made her new. He can do the same for you or someone you know.

My husband Al and I implore you to read, pray, and act. We know this book has changed our perspective on abuse. This is truly a story of *Hidden Bruises in Holy Places*.

Lisa Robertson
West Monroe, Louisiana

Lisa is the wife of Al Robertson, pastor at Whites Ferry Road Church in West Monroe. Lisa and Al travel the world speaking about many things, including healthy marriages and ending abortion and the grief it causes. Al is one of the Robertson brothers, the pastor one, from the hit television series *Duck Dynasty*.

Prologue

"He has sent me to bind up the brokenhearted,
to proclaim freedom for the captives, and release from
the darkness for the prisoners" (Isaiah 61:1).

Abuse is an ugly word, one conjuring images I would rather forget. But I can't. Having lived in the nightmare of an abusive marriage for thirty years, I am well acquainted with the subject. My children and I were victims of horrible abuse at the hands of a minister, and I fiercely desire to expose this evil that, for too long, has plagued the church I love. There are no titles by my name stamping me as an expert on domestic abuse, but I have most definitely been educated through my experience. I have survived it, conquered it, and am now using my experience to expose it and help others suffering in abusive relationships. Having been a victim of abuse doesn't define who I am, but it has shaped what I have become: a victor. Hopefully I can inspire other victims to be victorious through the power of Jesus. If so, the pain of my story is not without purpose.

Although both males and females can be victims, and although different forms of domestic abuse exist, female marital/dating victimization is this book's focus. Sadly, a commonly cited statistic is that one in four women report being in an abusive or destructive intimate relationship or marriage. Think about this statistic as you look around your church. It's astounding. Based on my experience, I tend to believe it to be *higher* in the church.

Unfortunately, many times the church is not equipped to deal with abuse in a healthy way.

Friends, to foster change we must adopt a new way of thinking in our approach to dealing with domestic abuse in Christian relationships. I have heard too many women's tragic stories—stories far worse than mine. Glimpses of these stories are provided in this book. Each experience is different as each woman finds the strength to leave her relationship or maintains the determination to stay. Despite the differences, there are countless similarities, including the basic need to be heard and validated. Perhaps by sifting through the rubble of my broken past and portraying a picture of abuse, I can be a conduit for change and healing while creating a greater awareness of the occurrence of domestic abuse in the church.

Broken and needing restoration, victims and abusers alike must receive the healing touch and amazing grace of Jesus. If abuse isn't addressed and grace isn't extended, however, the brokenness will continue. Though it would be much more comfortable and immensely easier for me to stay safely hidden in the shelter and tranquility of my new life, I can't. If I don't strive to create change, I am a part of the failure—and I refuse to be that anymore. Extending grace to my abuser, I have forgiven him,

> **IF I DON'T STRIVE TO CREATE CHANGE, I AM A PART OF THE FAILURE—AND I REFUSE TO BE THAT ANYMORE.**

confirming in my heart that I do not write out of a spirit of vengeance nor a pronouncement of judgment upon his current spiritual state. God's grace is available for every human soul.

Trusting that God is guiding me in writing this book, my desire is for every word to be initiated by His Spirit because He is the author and perfecter of faith. As Scripture warns, "He who speaks from himself seeks his own glory" (John 7:18). My only desire is to honor and glorify my Lord. Therefore, my words must be from Him; otherwise, they are worthless.

All of us have experienced defining moments when we drew a line in the sand—a proclamation of faith that changed us forever. As a seven-year-old girl living in Arizona, I was awed by the majestic desert mountains vaulted against the night sky. One evening while admiring those grand structures of nature, I recalled the Bible verse where Jesus said if I possess faith as a mustard seed, I can move a mountain. In my childlike faith, I told the mountain to move. And I was convinced it did move—if ever so slightly. Calling to mind this moment many times through my adult life has been a source of comfort in dark times.

So here I am again, facing a mountain and telling it to move in the name of Jesus. I am certain I will face resistance. A scheme of Satan and evil in the guise of religion can't be exposed without resistance.

But I have faith this mountain also will move and become another defining moment.

Introduction

"Carry each other's burdens, and in this way you will fulfill the law of Christ" (Galatians 6:2).

Pray for Insight

Countless abuse victims need validation, hope, and Jesus' redeeming grace. Most assuredly, the church should be where these victims can go to find relief. Unfortunately, many times they can't. Yet if Christian women can't turn to the church in their greatest hour of need, where can they go? In this book I attempt to enlighten churches on what to look for regarding signs of abuse and how to help both victims and abusers. I also provide my ideas for implementing a protocol to aid the victim during her terrifying transition of leaving an abusive relationship.

This information challenges the church to think differently about saving a marriage at all costs. Abuse is more prevalent in the church than some might think—yes, even among ministers—and is a threat to the sanctity of Christian marriage and is highly destructive to the family unit God intended. The church must not shirk this God-ordained responsibility reflected in the following Scripture:

Is not this the kind of fasting I have chosen: to loose the chains of injustice and untie the cords of the yoke, to set the oppressed free and break every yoke?

Is it not to share your food with the hungry and to provide the poor wanderer with shelter—when you see the naked, to clothe them, and not to turn away from your own flesh and blood?

Then your light will break forth like the dawn, and your heal-
ing will quickly appear; then your righteousness will go before
you, and the glory of the Lord will be your rear guard.

Then you will call, and the Lord will answer; you will cry for
help, and he will say: "Here am I. If you do away with the yoke
of oppression, with the pointing finger and malicious talk, and
if you spend yourselves in behalf of the hungry and satisfy the
needs of the oppressed, then your light will rise in the darkness,
and your night will become like the noonday."

The Lord will guide you always; he will satisfy your needs in a
sun-scorched land and will strengthen your frame.

You will be like a well-watered garden, like a spring whose
waters never fail. Your people will rebuild the ancient ruins
and will raise up the age-old foundations; you will be called
Repairer of Broken Walls, Restorer of Streets with Dwellings
(Isaiah 58:6-12).

Although I would rather be writing a recipe book or a romance novel, I'm instead doing what I believe God has called me to do. I've attempted to write each section of my story chronologically, but conveying thirty years of abuse is difficult, and everything does not fit perfectly. Bear with me, however. I believe my story will make sense as it unfolds.

Finally, as you read about a subject of such magnitude, I ask you to pray for insight; pray for open eyes and an open heart; pray for grace; pray for the church; pray for me; and pray for victims and former victims around the world. I believe He will answer our prayers.

The Beginning of the End

"For God does speak—now one way, then another, though no one perceives it. In a dream, in a vision of the night, when deep sleep falls on people as they slumber in their beds" (Job 33:14, 15).

Awakening

As I approached the decrepit house shrouded in darkness, deep sadness engulfed me. Still, I was compelled to enter. This house was once a place of happiness, unity of spirit, familial love, laughter, and security. The tattered remains of splintered wood and weathered paint were accentuated by the gaping holes and broken glass in the windows. Having fallen into utter disrepair—empty, barren—and now merely a shadow looming in the darkness, the house somehow seemed to be patiently awaiting restoration to its once glorious original state.

Sensing something sacred upon entering this old place—almost as if I'd entered the sanctuary of some beloved ancient cathedral—I dared not disturb the solemn, almost deafening silence. I forged on, careful to preserve the reverence that seemed to linger from the past. Normally skittish by nature and given to imagining the worst scenarios, I was surprised I was somehow not afraid—somehow I knew I must continue exploring with courage, curiosity, and anticipation.

As if motivated by some unknown force, I climbed the stairs and emerged on the second-floor landing, an open space large enough to be a sitting area or loft. I became immediately aware this was the area of the house I was to closely, carefully analyze. Strewn with debris and dust, this space was the central hub of the house. Illuminating the dark space was a faint glimmer shining through a large window providing just enough light to continue my exploration. Though the rest of the house seemed dead, in this *one place* life existed in some fragile form: a precious piece of the past somehow survived. Here I would find what I was seeking, although I wouldn't know what it was until it was eventually revealed to me.

Lying on the floor in front of me was a grandfather clock, toppled on its back by some forceful blow from which it never recov-

THOUGH THE REST OF THE HOUSE SEEMED DEAD, IN THIS *ONE PLACE* LIFE EXISTED IN SOME FRAGILE FORM: A PRECIOUS PIECE OF THE PAST SOMEHOW SURVIVED.

ered. No one had bothered to put it back in place. Covered in dust and cobwebs, this once magnificent artifact faithfully kept its vigil of timekeeping as evidenced by the movement of its hands on its worn but majestic face. Though everything around it seemed lifeless, this clock was too stubborn to succumb to its surroundings. Though battered, it had survived.

Next I opened a door to discover a dark closet. Stacked inside were boxes with crushed and partially opened lids containing cherished treasures I recognized as contributions of my father and mother that I'd stored away. At the same time, I somehow meant to keep them close at hand and accessible when needed. Comfortingly familiar, I loved each precious memento, and the closet seemed to provide a safe space where I could feel at peace.

On the other side of the stairway I spotted a large room. Inside, a glaring floodlight hung suspended over a table—a vivid contrast to the shadows throughout the rest of the house. Seated at the table was a group of men I didn't recognize. I overheard one of them ask, "What should we do about her?" Puzzled, I thought, *About 'her'? About me? Am I the topic of their discussion?* Seemingly prohibited from entering the room, I listened with curiosity to the serious conversation from my spot just outside the door.

Just then a young man I'd known since I was a young girl appeared on the stairs. Familiar and close to my heart—though many years had passed since I last saw him—his strikingly handsome face was just as I remembered it. He was beautiful. His entrance both comforting and surprising, my heart nearly burst with excitement at the sight of him. The prince of my heart when I was young, he embodied my every dream of love. As he drew near, his face and demeanor revealed he was on a mission. He passed me on the landing as if I wasn't there. He entered the room to join the men at the table and declared, "I know her, and I know what to do."

A FRANK AND UNFEIGNED REFLECTION OF MYSELF, THIS DREAM WAS GOD'S REVELATION TO ME— AN HONEST PROBE INTO MY HEART, MY SOUL, AND MY LIFE, AND ALL THAT HAD BEEN LOST.

Abruptly, I awoke. It was all just a dream—a mysterious dream. Overwhelmed with emotion and weeping uncontrollably in the dark, I tried to make sense of this strange vision. What did it mean? Why was I so profoundly moved by it? Then, as if by divine insight, I understood. Having been afraid to see the dream's significance before and unprepared to handle it, I was beginning to comprehend its meaning. A frank and unfeigned reflection of myself, this dream was God's revelation to me—an honest probe into my heart, my soul, and my life, and all that had been lost.

I was the disheveled and shabby house in the darkness— empty, abandoned, and void of life—a mere shell of the person I once was. The landing at the top of the staircase represented my heart, worn by years of domestic abuse. Still dutifully keeping time in its prostrate position, the grandfather clock represented my spirit: damaged, yet still striving to keep the faith while everything around me appeared dark and hopeless. The closet symbolized the chamber of my heart guarding the precious memories of my childhood and my parents' teachings and wisdom. The discussion at the table reflected a deep examination into my broken soul, illuminating the realization I needed to be restored. The young man to the rescue—all I ever knew of true love when I was a young girl—represented the love I was missing all those years.

So much was taken. So much was given away until there was nothing left to give. Now emotionally emaciated and spiritually bankrupt, I was nearly demolished—much like the old house.

With this dream I began the journey of restoration, the tedious task of finding who I once was—the person God made me to be—the one I lost in trying to become what someone else expected me to be. After twenty-seven years of living in abuse, I discerned a faint light trickling into the windows of my soul. Revealing to me the necessity of my utter dependence upon Him, God sent me this dream so I could begin the process of deciding how to take control of my life.

Just before the dream, a friend of mine offered his perception of my marriage: "Seems to me you were sold into slavery." Although I was offended and vehemently denied his comment's blatant truth, something inside me changed. Unlocking an iron dungeon door sealed shut all those years, my friend's words led to this dream only a few days later. So began the long process of taking stock of my life, attempting to find my voice and establish boundaries, and eventually deciding to leave the marriage three years later—after my husband had nearly killed us both.

By God's grace, I survived to tell my story. Evidence of His astounding grace permeates every word of it.

Marital Abuse

"The LORD is a refuge for the oppressed,
a stronghold in times of trouble" (Psalm 9:9).

Beginnings

February 12, 1983. My wedding day. An avalanche of emotions ravaged my 18-year-old heart, mind, soul, and body because I knew a sentence of doom was about to be pronounced upon my life. Despite being abused by my fiancé during our engagement, I was unaware those experiences had a name. Unable to articulate them, how could I expect others to understand? I wanted to scream, but I was afraid no one would listen to or recognize the magnitude of my despair. Helpless to change my course, I stood dutifully at the marriage altar in silence, sinking deeper into the darkest pit imaginable.

My life had not always been this miserable. I came from a loving, churchgoing, upper-middle-class family. My precious mother was a wonderful homemaker, tremendous cook, my best friend, and the person I vehemently argued with the most. Entering the ministry when I was in high school, my dad was loving and full of fun, but strict. I adored him. Having been a bit of a wild thing when he was young, Dad was determined my younger brother and I did not follow in his footsteps. Though perhaps a bit overly strict, Dad was a good father and did the best he could to lead his family in love. He provided a stable homelife, and for this I have always been grateful.

Especially strict regarding boys, Dad did not allow me to date until I was 18. Boys could call and come to the house, or we could go places together with my parents or the high school youth group; this established the extent of my dating life. I didn't always agree with the rules, but I abided by them.

When I was about 15, boys came crawling out of the woodwork. I was pretty and outgoing, and I laughed a lot. I had come into my own. Dad, however, was relentless in enforcing his rules.

Unable to meet my father's expectations for a suitable match for his daughter, many young men came and went.

A few years earlier, when I was only 12, an older boy caught my attention. It was the mid-'70s, and the roller-skating rink with the disco ball was all the rage—the place to go on Sunday nights with the church youth group. At a rink in Lubbock, Texas, I met Brett, the most handsome creation I'd ever seen. Smitten as if struck by a lightning bolt, I saw stars. The disco music and the swirling diamond-like reflections from the suspended ball overhead spectacularly collided, creating the perfect backdrop for love. Brett, on the other hand, showed no interest in a gangly, awkward 12-year-old girl with bobby pins in her bangs and freckles on her nose.

He looked at me differently, however, when I ran into him at a softball game a few years later. I was 15 then and no longer an awkward, freckle-faced girl; I'd undergone the proverbial transformation from ugly duckling to a swan. This time Brett was the one struck by the lightning bolt, and it was off to the races for both of us. Wild and beautiful, this love experience was all I ever dreamed it would be. I couldn't eat. I dreamt about him by night and swooned over him by day. Lovesick was an understatement. I had it bad, and so did he. Seemingly, there was no stopping this train and where it was bound. A 19-year-old boy with a plan that included me, Brett didn't care how long he had to wait or what obstacle he had to overcome to be with me.

Dad's strict rules didn't deter Brett in his pursuit. Night after night he came to my house and just sat there watching TV with my parents and me. If we were lucky, we would sometimes have the living room to ourselves. Surprisingly, my dad let Brett drive me to youth group functions and movies with my friends. Sometimes I could meet him at the mall where he worked, Kinney Shoes—the old go-to shoe place from the mall's '70s glory days. I can still picture how adorable he looked with his tie, black slacks, and nametag. While going to college, he worked to support himself and send money home to his siblings. A kid from a less than ideal homelife, he wanted to provide for his brother and sister. Brett was a good guy, and I loved him. Never questioning my dad's rules, he treated me honorably and respected my ambitions, my commitment to Jesus, and my moral standards.

Brett and I planned to get married after I graduated high school and spent two years in the mission field. This would give him time to complete college and seminary school and enter the ministry. My life's goal was to do mission work and marry a minister. In my teenage mind, my dream was starting to unfold. Head over heels in love, we were going to get married; it was just a matter of time.

He even gave me a little diamond ring to seal the deal.

However, feeling we were too young for such a relationship, Dad was understandably unnerved. In trying to do what was best for me, he strongly advised that Brett and I end our romance. Bless Dad's heart and his protective instinct. He had the best intentions.

Never fully recovering from the breakup, I thought of Brett often over the years, especially on October 19, his birthday. Grieving the loss, I detached myself from those feelings and rambled through the next year of my life. I remained the dutiful daughter, witty friend, and "good girl"; I learned to be what others needed me to be. Sometimes I wonder if those attributes, combined with my broken heart trying to mend, was a large part of the reason I married the person I did. In a misguided attempt to please God and other people, I accepted whatever came, disregarding my feelings as if they were a weakness. At times, though, I would allow myself to embrace those sweet memories of young love embodied in a boy named Brett.

While I was floating through the clouds in my relationship with Brett, Dad met the man I would eventually marry—a different type of man, a different story, a different outcome. He and Dad were preaching together at the same seminar, and for Dad it was future son-in-law love at first sight. He came home singing the praises of what seemed to be a genuine Prince Charming—the first guy to receive my dad's complete approval. After breaking up with Brett and hearing from others some incredible reports about this man, I was excited, naturally, to meet him.

We met the next spring at a Christian gathering of about ten thousand people. He was tall, dark, and handsome—not the kind of person who could be overlooked, even in such a large crowd. I spotted him before I knew who he was. Flashing his dazzling smile when Dad introduced us, this young man said, "I've been wanting to meet you." It was *game over* for me. I was hooked—at least for the moment. I was 16; he was 28. The meeting changed my life forever.

Mesmerized by his charm, words, and compliments, my family, most of my friends, and I were spellbound—a phenomenon often called the "halo effect." His charismatic personality blinded us from seeing the real person behind the glimmer. I was extremely infatuated during the three days we spent at the seminar. I kept thinking, *Is he real? Is he an angel?* I decided I was going to marry him. A gorgeous man and extremely charming minister, one who seemingly could quote the Bible backward and forward, he met all the criteria. Excitedly, I went home and announced my plans to Dad, who was thrilled. Both of us were suckered in.

We exchanged a few letters over the following months; this man's words were like poetry to me. His letters portrayed someone nearly perfect. With no opportunity to see him in everyday life, I fell in love with a dream created by flowery words and gushy sentiment.

After seeing him one more time in June of that year at another Christian gathering, I received one more letter. Then there was silence for months, and this caused me to wonder, *What did I do wrong? What did I say?* Did he decide I wasn't pretty enough? Was I too pushy? Maybe I just wasn't good enough. Questioning my worth in response to his silence should have been a warning sign that this was not a healthy relationship. Having seen him only twice, I didn't have much time invested.

I should have realized my feelings were only a crush when I got over him quickly and moved on with life—this splitting was no comparison to what I felt for Brett. Then, when he called about seven months later wanting to know if I was going to the seminar where we had first met a year earlier, I was stunned. With the crush coming over me once more, I told him I would be there.

What happened next is a blur. All I know is when I came home from the seminar, I learned he asked my dad if he could marry me. When he proposed the following month, I accepted. I seemed to wake up one day engaged to a stranger I'd only spent time with on three occasions—and I wasn't even sure how it happened.

WHAT HAPPENED NEXT IS A BLUR. ALL I KNOW IS WHEN I CAME HOME FROM THE SEMINAR, I LEARNED HE ASKED MY DAD IF HE COULD MARRY ME.

The proposal wasn't at all the romantic experience I'd envisioned as a little girl. Having gone to visit him in his home state of Louisiana, I was standing in his mother's kitchen stuffing myself with smoked turkey from the fridge late one night after everyone was in bed. Upon entering the room, he announced he wanted to ask me something. It was as if, while brushing his teeth, he decided he might need to ask me to marry him. He never said "I love you" or "I need you" or even "Will you marry me?" With no romantic forethought, no engagement ring, no getting down on one knee, his proposal consisted of asking me to put aside my plans of going to the mission field to help him in his ministry instead— it was more like the announcement of a ministry partnership than a marriage proposal. I could help *him*—what a thought! Embedded in the proposal was the premise of our relationship for the rest of our lives: *what I could do to help him.*

* * * * *

In the months that followed I began to see behaviors that frightened me—warning signs that should have prevented me from marrying him. However, his mind games already having begun, he used a tactic called *gaslighting*: psychologically manipulating me into questioning my actions, my reasoning, and my sanity. For example, making unfounded accusations about me, he was very persuasive and made me question myself, and this resulted in my apologizing for things I didn't do. He gained control over me, and this was evidenced early in our relationship when he became enraged discovering my family's small dog slept with me on top of the bed covers. Slinging the covers off the bed and shaking them violently, he insisted no wife of his would sleep with a dog. Despite being frightened by his angry outburst and bizarre behavior, I remained in the relationship.

Throughout our engagement, his explosive temper erupted frequently; I never knew what was going to set him off. One day a simple conversation we were having abruptly turned violent. Out of nowhere he began yelling, punched the top of my dad's vehicle that we were standing next to, and stormed off. Having never seen such behavior before, I was scared and, consequently, broke the engagement. Being a master manipulator, though, he went forward at church, asked for prayer, cried, and said all the right words to change my mind. With onlookers waiting to see what my decision would be, I felt pressured to accept his apology and agreed to resume the engagement.

Attempting to break the engagement three more times, I was always persuaded—or manipulated—to keep my commitment. Several times I was erroneously advised it was God's will I marry him. Young and incredibly naïve, I was convinced, as were others, that breaking up was just a knee-jerk reaction to a relationship's normal ups and downs. Because abuse is such a tangled web of deceit, mind control, and manipulation, I couldn't make sense of it all or articulate my feelings and experiences.

> **BECAUSE ABUSE IS SUCH A TANGLED WEB OF DECEIT, MIND CONTROL, AND MANIPULATION, I COULDN'T MAKE SENSE OF IT ALL OR ARTICULATE MY FEELINGS AND EXPERIENCES.**

As my wedding day drew nearer, a feeling of doom overwhelmed me, and even my family became concerned about his behavior. Two nights before the wedding he instructed me to iron a shirt for him. Knowing all I still needed to do for the wedding, my mother and grandmother offered to iron the shirt instead. He angrily responded, however, that no one would be ironing his shirt but me. I was going to be his wife, and he would be making the decisions about my chores. If he wanted me to do something, I was going to do it—without question. My mom struggled with his assertion; this was all a foreshadowing of the agony to come for my entire family, and the effect his behavior would have on their lives.

A couple of days later I sealed my fate. Feeling as though I was being sent to the guillotine and unable to bring myself to back out, I put on a happy face and walked down the aisle. Even now, feelings of hopelessness hang heavily over my mind as I revisit that day so long ago.

After the wedding, when the photographer asked us to kiss for a photo, my new husband quipped, "Yes, she's mine now." I remember wanting to retaliate against the comment, which seemed to suggest I had become his property. Although sickened, I rationalized that he didn't mean it. He did.

I won't embarrass you or myself by detailing the wedding night and honeymoon. Being naïve and shy when it came to the subject of sex, I didn't know what to expect. Suffice it to say it was the beginning of the mental/emotional/sexual abuse, manipulation, coercion, and fear that defined sex for me for the next thirty years.

Newlywed

The first few months of my marriage were extremely difficult. Immediately after our wedding, my husband moved us to Illinois, leaving my family and most of my friends behind in Texas. With little income and expensive long-distance rates, phone calls were restricted. I felt isolated, as though on a deserted island—the ideal circumstance for abuse to flourish—and I had no one to witness or object. My only reality was the one my husband created, and it provided the perfect environment for mind control to take root and flourish. With my husband my only companion, most of my ties with friends were severed. And with limited family interaction, I became a full-blown victim early in our marriage.

Desperately lonely, some days I sat crying for hours. Women in the church were kept at arm's length. Warning me about the influence they might have on me because they weren't "spiritual" enough, my husband wouldn't permit me to create friendships or socialize with them. When they planned a wedding shower for us, he threw a fit before we arrived. He made us an hour and a half late and wouldn't let me call with an explanation. When we finally arrived, only the few hostesses remained. The situation was awkward, but we posed for pictures and smiled as though nothing was wrong. Thinking about the charade even today, I feel sick. I'm certain people wondered about the odd circumstances surrounding our visit. Yet no one said a word about it or about my sheltered existence in general.

I remained reclusive, constructing walls of protection to guard against disclosure of my life's mounting secrets.

Concerned for my emotional and physical well-being, my mother came for a visit to check on me a few weeks after my wedding. She grieved not only my absence but also her silence regarding her intuition about the relationship—and not intervening—before I married. She suspected something was amiss, but unfortunately her concerns were not confirmed until it was too late. When she arrived, my husband was on his best behavior until one day when Mom wanted to buy a pair of lamps for our sparsely furnished living room. When we got to the store, he announced she could buy me only one lamp. His announcement was simply a power trip. He wanted to emphasize his control reigned supreme and that the ultimate authority in decision-making was his. Although relatively inconsequential, the episode was indicative of his future dealings with my mother and other

I REMAINED RECLUSIVE, CONSTRUCTING WALLS OF PROTECTION TO GUARD AGAINST DISCLOSURE OF MY LIFE'S MOUNTING SECRETS.

family members. His behavior worsened to the point that he eventually physically threatened my dad and brother as well as his own brother. Crazy, I know, but true. For my mother, fears regarding my abusive husband unfortunately became her nightmare.

Increased Victimization

As the months passed, my husband was prone to insane raging, screaming, punching holes in walls and car windshields, throwing and breaking items, and leaving destruction in his wake. At times after these episodes he would disappear until the wee hours of the morning with no explanation of where he had been. As he grew more violent with me, I dared not ask questions.

About four months into our marriage, my husband decided to move to Memphis to attend graduate school to study biblical theology. During the moving process we stayed with family. Those few weeks before arriving in Memphis were a nightmare during which I saw signs that dashed any hope of ever having a normal marriage.

We visited his parents in Louisiana first, and they immediately took me clothes shopping. I didn't realize how much weight I had lost until I saw the looks on their faces. In the four stressful months since my wedding, I had eaten sporadically. My nerves always on edge, and my stomach in knots, my desire for food was severely inhibited. As a result, I weighed just over 100 pounds, and my clothes were hanging off my 5-foot-6-inch frame. Eating became another dimension of my life that I allowed my husband to control. Sometimes when I was "in trouble," I knew not to eat for fear I would exacerbate the situation. My husband didn't like it if I enjoyed eating while he was brooding about some infraction he perceived I had committed. Consequently, during the shopping trip with his mother, I was shocked to discover I'd dwindled from a size 9 to a size 1—completely indicative of the effect of stress.

During the week at his parents' home, everyone did what he demanded. Everything went his way—or else. I saw him scream at and berate his mom and dad more than once. We were all victims—one as sick as the other, allowing his insane behavior to continue. At one point during our visit I witnessed one of his most demonic displays. Irate with me because I misunderstood one of his requests, he began growling and seething and spewing curse words at me and punching himself in the face, causing his lip to bleed and cheek to swell. A nauseating reminder of the horrific day still hangs on his mother's wall—a photograph taken the next day clearly displaying his swollen cheek and visibly puffy lip outlining his forced smile.

While we were in Louisiana my dad came from Texas for a couple of days to speak at a conference. My visit with him was short but sweet, and I think he sensed things were not right in my life. When we took him to the airport to head home, he and my husband got into a theological debate. Joining the conversation, I agreed with my dad on the subject. When Dad had left, I paid dearly for siding with my dad's interpretation. My husband stormed out of the airport ahead of me, and as I got to the car, he began screaming at me, exclaiming I was never to disagree with him or side with anyone else—especially my dad. As we exited the airport parking lot, he drove like a madman, squealing tires and throwing a hubcap in the process. Afraid and hopeless, I wanted my daddy to return and rescue me.

When we finally left my in-laws' home a week later, we planned to arrive in Texas that night to visit my family. Planning a celebration complete with a special home-cooked meal upon our arrival, my mom invited some members from my home church, wonderful people I loved dearly. I couldn't wait to see them and be home for the first time since the wedding.

Having seen some ghastly displays of my husband's foul mood in the two weeks we were in Louisiana, I dreaded the drive to Texas and feared what might happen. Confirming my misgivings, he yelled and spouted bizarre and rude comments to his parents as we were leaving the house. His dad just stood there and cried. Despite my fears, I kept thinking that at least I would be safe at home with my parents by nightfall. I was sadly mistaken. After driving a couple of hours, he became irate with me although I'd said or done nothing since we left Louisiana.

During his tirade he devoured a plum like an animal, letting the juice run down his chin, and then bellowed a hideously evil laugh. Convinced he was possessed, I was terrified.

Suddenly, he decided not to complete the trip. He didn't care that my mom planned a dinner party and was awaiting our arrival or that a crowd of people was expecting to see me. Pulling off the interstate, he drove to a hotel and forbade me to call anyone. Neither of our parents knew where we were, if we were safe, or if he'd done something stupid. Quite literally a hostage, I wasn't allowed to leave the room or speak to him, and I ate nothing. I only went to the bathroom with his approval. Although I didn't realize it then, he'd committed a felony: false imprisonment. Imprisoned in every sense of the word, I didn't know what he would do next. Anxious the entire evening, my parents hosted the dinner party without us.

Late the next day, he finally phoned his mother and told her where we were. After hearing his demented comments, she phoned a family friend who called the hotel and informed my husband the police were contacted and on their way. Determined not to be there when officers arrived, he demanded we flee.

I was relieved to be back in the car, but the relief was short-lived when, after traveling a few miles, we stopped at another hotel, where he expected sex. I felt fearfully compelled to act like nothing was wrong and fulfill his wishes. In my thinking this was a moment of relief and a sick sort of tenderness from him in the midst of the insanity. I find it difficult to explain what this sort of abuse does to the mind. (The memory being so completely traumatic, it was blocked from my mind until recently when I wrote about this disgusting episode.) In fact, it's still traumatic. Full of despair, I was trying to appease him. A one-day trip had been extended to three days, and I wanted to get home to my mama and daddy.

After I performed my "duty," his mood changed, and he decided we could continue our trip. He allowed me to call my parents under strict supervision and menacing instructions not to divulge any information about the past couple of days. No matter what questions they asked or how concerned they were, I was forced to act like nothing was wrong. As I hung up the phone he began yelling that I had revealed too much information. Overcome with fear and not knowing what he would do next, I began trembling uncontrollably, even whimpering pitifully. Something about my response brought him

THE BOND CREATED BETWEEN VICTIM AND ABUSER—CAPTIVE AND CAPTOR—WAS BEING FORMED.

back to the reality of the torture I'd experienced the previous few days. In a sick and manipulative sort of way, he hugged me and told me everything was going to be all right. The message was that the trauma he had brought on me was over, and the hug was a gesture of what a hero he was. My tortured mind told me he wasn't such a bad person, that he had just experienced a bad couple of days. The bond created between victim and abuser—captive and captor—was being formed. We loaded our vehicle and traveled the rest of the way to my parents' home.

Exhausted from the trauma of the trip, I was overcome with relief when we pulled into my parents' driveway. Though I was not allowed to reveal the details of the events of the past few days, I nevertheless exposed some of them later in a private conversation with my mom; I explained how I could not call or leave the room. However, I did not tell her about the sexual abuse, the limited amount of food I'd consumed over the previous few days, or police being called to the hotel. Not understanding the full extent of what I was actually revealing, I surprisingly conveyed to her my feelings of being a captive—confused and afraid. In retrospect, I see it as somewhat comparable to Patty Hearst and her well-known 1970s account of being held captive. Yet, in nearly the same breath, I excused his behavior. The conversation haunted my mother for years. In a stern exchange with my momentarily "repentant" husband, my dad warned him he would come get me if a similar episode ever happened again. In truth, though, I'd already begun hiding, enabling, and excusing. Self-deception brought on by the trauma and brainwashing became the most comfortable existence for me, so my parents couldn't help me. I just wanted to forget the past few weeks and enjoy the time with my family.

Being the classic victim, I developed the characteristics of Stockholm Syndrome, a psychological phenomenon whereby victims develop sympathy, loyalty, affection, and compassion toward their captors/abusers/abductors. A survival strategy, this syndrome lessens the trauma of being a victim and the punishment for being disobedient. I normalized otherwise psychotic behavior, making the situation more acceptable in my mind. Psychological abuse is a curious phenomenon. Because of the trauma, I obeyed without question and automatically diffused feelings of conflict or disagreement. I gradually began losing touch with reality, and as time passed, I became increasingly convinced my husband was right and everyone else was wrong. My mentality—combined with my commitment to marriage and to what I thought was God's will—held me captive for so many years.

Becoming a Superwoman

Within a few weeks of our trip to Texas, we moved to Memphis, and there I grew increasingly despondent with each passing day. However, I did get a part-time job as a teacher's aide at a Christian school, and this helped ease the torture and pay the rent. While going to graduate school, my husband worked part time at Federal Express until he was invited to work with the youth in the church we were attending. We lived on about eight hundred dollars a month. Looking back on those difficult years, I'm not sure how we made it, but God always provided. Despite my increasingly difficult circumstances, His faithful provision remained evident.

Besides working at the school, I tried to become even more of what my husband expected. While he attended graduate school, I was the editor and typist of all of his papers and his thesis—not an easy feat with a portable Smith-Corona typewriter and only one year of a high school typing class. I did all the cooking, cleaning, and laundry. He helped with none of the chores. In addition, I worked to ensure I was the best youth minister's wife I could be. Not even 20 years old, I became a multitasking superwoman.

It seemed the more I became what I thought my husband wanted, the more frequent and physical his rages became, including shoving me to the ground and locking me in rooms. The mental and emotional abuse was maddening, and I never knew what each day would bring.

Walking on eggshells while trying to stay a step ahead of his anger was exhausting. The fear and isolation became unbearable, and I frequently experienced bouts of depression. His disappearances also became more frequent.

One morning after he'd been gone all night, I went out to the car and found his wedding ring in the ashtray. I was dumbfounded. When I asked him about it, he was evasive; he'd obviously been up to no good. I knew not to press the issue, so the reason for his disappearance remained a mystery. Having become the poster child for codependency and enabling, I never asked about the incident again. He was never forced to account for anything he wasn't willing to.

The Cycle

In the midst of our destructive marriage, there were some moments of relief when things went well. In a sad way, though, the good times only made the situation more torturous because I wanted to hold on to every good second before the madness inevitably began again. This pattern is part of the abuse cycle.

In the cycle's first phase, I felt the tension building. Because of fear, I felt the need to pacify him—a futile attempt to divert impending disaster. My stomach in knots, I would tremble as though having a panic attack. I knew what was coming next.

The next phase, the "incident," involved explosions of rage, intimidation, threats, destruction of items, and physical violence. I saw his evil grimace and heard his growl. Acting like a maniac, he would grab me, push me, and scream in my face. After these incidents, which were like cyclones striking their victims, I spent the next hours putting the house back in order—cleaning up glass and broken items, filling trash bins with destroyed articles, repositioning furniture, and sometimes doctoring wounds I received from flying debris.

During the next phase, the reconciliation stage, he would switch personalities and become sweet and docile: buying me extravagant gifts, bringing me flowers, or taking me to a special restaurant to "apologize" for his actions. All the while he passive-aggressively blamed me by making such comments as "I'm sorry, but you just pushed me." Yet he'd just showered me with gifts, making me think, *Maybe it really was my fault.* In the process I became even more attached to him. The mind games were incredible, causing me to doubt myself and believe I was the crazy one. In reality, I was slowly being driven crazy. A master at this phase, my husband's reconciliation attempts convinced me his behavior was not so bad after all.

Then came the calm phase, the "honeymoon period," when all seemed right with the world; I tried to convince myself the madness wouldn't reoccur. I made him special meals and genuinely enjoyed time with him, wishing life would always be so pleasant. However, I knew I was fooling myself, and my fears always resurfaced. Although trying to suppress my concerns to enjoy the peaceful moment while it lasted, I knew it wouldn't. It never did.

Then the cycle began again, and it worsened progressively. Over time I became increasingly physically, mentally, and spiritually exhausted with days turning into months and months into years while the stress took a toll on my body. At times I vomited in response. After one of my husband's raging outbursts, I vomited three times in one night; still, he said nothing and showed no concern. When I got up for church the next morning, he sat up in bed, snapped his fingers at me, and ordered me to get back in bed. Still brooding, he wasn't going to let me go to church. I knew I must obey. Neither of us went—even though he was working with the church's youth group. I'm sure he provided the excuse we weren't feeling well. Truly, I wasn't.

In the early stages of my marriage, this continuous cycle of abuse adversely affected my health. I began having bouts of irregular female bleeding. At first, the bleeding was just spotting a few days a month. Over time, however, I bled for thirty days at a time, would stop for a week, and then began again. Because doctors couldn't do much without desperate measures, I lived with this condition.

In research I found this condition resulted from trauma and constant stress. My husband must have known he was causing the stress. In fact, in the middle of one of his rants, he began screaming "Bleed!!" It was as though he was invoking a curse over me. I didn't fully recover from this condition until more than thirty years later—after I left the marriage and began healing.

Temporary Shelter

Although only 19, I lived an emotional and mental lifetime in the short few months I'd been married. I was caught in a constantly whirling cycle of strategically planning what to say or not say, how to smile or not smile, how to think or not think. Abuse wears the mind and body very thin—so much so that I wondered if I could ever recover. I rode an emotional roller coaster hoping not to tumble. But I always did, crashing and burning in the aftermath of consequences.

On one of the particularly bad days filled with rage, torment, and mind games, I took a walk just to gather myself and find peace. Desperate to escape for a while, I felt drawn to a row of bushes along the edge of a field in the distance. Seeking shelter from the chaos and wanting to feel secure, I crawled into an opening of a large bush. It began to rain. Sitting in my leafy shelter, I felt cheated by life—all my dreams and spirit crushed by the weight of abuse. I remember the sound of the rain plopping on the leaves around me. The buzz of the traffic in the distance saddened me because it reminded me how the world was such a big place with so many people, yet I was so alone and afraid. I was left

> **SITTING IN MY LEAFY SHELTER, I FELT CHEATED BY LIFE—ALL MY DREAMS AND SPIRIT CRUSHED BY THE WEIGHT OF ABUSE.**

to only think, *Does anyone know or care I'm here?* I felt helpless and overwhelmed while thinking of my bleak future. Living in constant darkness wreaked havoc with my mind and spirit and required unimaginable strength and energy to cope until the next bout of my husband's insanity.

At the same time, the smell of dirt and decaying leaves mixed with the scent of rain somehow comforted me, perhaps reminding me of happier times and childhood joys. I began searching for an answer and a glimmer of hope while huddled in my bush, and I suddenly experienced something profound, something comparable to Moses' hearing God's voice from a burning bush. Louder than the voice of despair and fear in my heart, I heard God say, "I am with you. Don't be afraid. You can handle this." Something about the moment changed me. I found a determination of spirit that hadn't existed before, a sense I was going to be okay. Out of my sanctuary of leaves and dirt, I emerged stronger. Though there would be more excruciating battles to face, and many defeats to endure, my bush experience increased my tenacity and intensified my resolve to keep fighting.

It was a defining moment I have never forgotten. Sitting in that bush, I learned I possessed a special gift of joy, which God reaffirmed through the experience. Neither Satan nor my husband could ever *completely* steal my joy. Though I experienced moments I thought it was gone, it always returned. God instilled in me an extra measure of joy from the moment of my birth, and my dad raised me to be strong in will and strong in Jesus. The combination of joy and strength kept me holding on.

Minister's Wife

Three years into my marriage, just before my first son was born, we moved to a small town in South Texas where my husband became the church's pulpit minister, his first head pastor job. Only 21, I traversed the tedious and stressful maze of responsibilities of a minster's wife while walking the fragile and ever-narrowing tightrope of abuse. Thankfully, it was a small church with loving people. I loved the ministry, and I loved the people, some who I remain in contact with to this day. The people of the church there will never know what solace they provided me and what blessings their love and support were.

From the outside, my situation appeared, to others, to be dreamy. But sadly, during this time my enabling behavior became a sickness. I was compelled to hide the insanity. Our livelihood depended on it, and it was nice having a beautiful parsonage (preacher's home) and a small but consistent salary. I wanted to be what the congregation expected and what I thought I was supposed to be. To ensure the illusion lasted, I put on a happy face and kept up the appearances of a dutiful minister's wife.

One day not long after we moved to Texas, my husband left without telling me where he was going or when he would return. I was concerned because my first son's due date was imminent. He left anyway. When he returned, I learned he flew to Chicago for no apparent reason. I have no idea what he did there and, as usual, I didn't demand an explanation. In fact, upon his return, I dressed up and made a special meal complete with china and candles and even tied a bow around our new puppy's neck—gestures that, in essence, rewarded my husband for leaving.

Convincing myself he must get away because I wasn't good enough, I was determined to be a better wife—enabling behavior at its finest.

Transitions

Two months into our Texas ministry, my first son, John, was born. As many women do, I thought having a baby would help solve some of my marriage's dysfunctional issues. But my thoughts could not have been further from the truth. Instead, the dysfunction worsened, and the abuse spilled over to my son. I learned to cope the best I could and tried to focus on keeping peace for me and my baby boy.

Our stay in Texas lasted only eighteen months. In fact, we never stayed anywhere very long. My husband didn't like being accountable to anyone for anything—especially his sin. After renting a pornographic movie in our small-town video store, he was afraid he would be found out. So we packed our belongings. After repairing holes my husband's fist created in the walls, we left. Our sudden departure from Texas hurt and stunned the church members, indicating how well our façade had been maintained.

With no job and no income, we moved from our beautiful home in Texas to Louisiana—circumstances like these would become our norm. I was never sure if my husband was going to be employed or if he would decide to move or make a reckless financial decision. Establishing roots was impossible. I tried to make each new place a home, and I slowly became numb to the pain of detachment. Eventually I learned not to allow myself to become emotionally attached to people or places.

In Louisiana we moved into a wretched apartment we rented on a weekly basis. Like something from a horror movie, it was one in a small row of apartments in the country with no other neighbors. Entering the apartment the first night and turning on the lights, we saw hundreds of roaches infesting the wall; they actually gave the illusion of wallpaper. Since our furniture was in storage, my baby son slept in a playpen. My sleep was troubled as I thought of roaches crawling on him. Looking back, I should have taken my son and slept in the car. After we set off pesticide bombs the next day, I swept up huge mounds of dead roaches. The pesticide was only partially successful, so the next day we set off more bombs. As I swept up more heaps of roaches, more continued to appear. In time, I would just learn to live with the awful creatures.

When our small amount of money ran out, we prepared to live in our car. However, the day the rent was due, we miraculously received a check in the mail, and this allowed us another week in our creepy apartment, which was better than the alternative. The following week my husband finally took my in-laws up on their offer for us to stay with them until we could get established. If not for them, we would have been homeless and had nothing to eat. Not only providing us a place to live, they also paid for our necessities and graciously gave us a thousand dollars.

It was during this time that my husband orchestrated one of his most bizarre, selfish, deceitful, and manipulative stunts of our marriage. Taking the money his parents gave us, he announced he was leaving without saying where he was going or how long he would be gone. Since this incident was before cell phones, we could not track him. After a week of his absence, I finally received a collect phone call from a stranger, a preacher at a Florida church. "I have your husband here with me," the man said, "and he is ready to come home. But he requests upon his return there be no questions asked or explanations required about his activities the last few days." First, who is brazen enough to appear at a church and convince a complete stranger to make such a phone call? Second, who is audacious enough to make such a request of his wife and mother after he has taken a thousand dollars and gone gallivanting in Florida? And third, what preacher in his right mind would agree to make such a call? This was a perfect example of my husband's mind-controlling power—even with complete strangers. What's worse, I abided by this request. I must have been out of my mind. The years of suppression had transformed me into a virtual robot, obeying my husband's requests without question. Exacerbating the craziness, my mother-in-law, despite knowing he'd taken her money, followed his request as well. When he returned home, life went on as if normal—with no questions asked.

We stayed three years in Louisiana, where my husband ran a lawn care service, and we eventually rented a tiny house

WITHOUT HAVING THE MINISTRY ON WHICH TO FOCUS, I WAS EXTREMELY LONELY AND UNFULFILLED— EXCEPT FOR MY BOND WITH MY PRECIOUS YOUNG SON. I HATED LOUISIANA.

across town from my in-laws. He also started preaching part-time at a small church about two hours away. However, after a short time, he abruptly decided to leave the church when discord arose because the members didn't agree with his view on a theological issue. Without having the ministry on which to focus, I was extremely lonely and unfulfilled—except for my bond with my precious young son. I hated Louisiana. Repeatedly through the years, when money or jobs ran out, Louisiana was our go-to place to live since my husband was born and raised there. I have dear friends there, but Louisiana is too much of a reminder of miserable years of abuse.

Abuse of My Family

Near the end of 1990, after three years in Louisiana, we returned to the ministry, for which I was grateful. Pregnant with my second son, Seth, I welcomed a steady income and perhaps some accountability for my husband. He decided he wanted to move to Texas to help my father's inner-city ministry in San Antonio—not an arrangement which thrilled my father, who had already experienced my husband's controlling tendencies. Feeling forced and manipulated into accepting my husband's partnership in the ministry, my father tried to make the best of it. He was encouraged knowing his daughter and grandsons would be near.

Supplying financial support, a small church in Arkansas requested we live and minister there for a year before they sent us to San Antonio. Since Seth was born just before we moved to Arkansas, I now mothered two sons under five while becoming reacquainted with ministerial responsibilities. The year in Arkansas is a blur to me except for the memories of some precious people I grew to love there.

We finally moved to San Antonio in December 1991. Although I was happy to live in the same city as my parents, the relationship between my husband and my family collapsed during the year we spent there. I believe my husband intended to gain control of my father's ministry to persuade church members to conform to his authority. Pressuring my father, he constantly threatened that my sons and I would be alienated from him and my mother if my father didn't heed his wishes.

Almost immediately upon our move to San Antonio, my husband began implementing strategies to ensure the small church's members would perceive him as the head minister.

Through his charisma and brainwashing tactics, he began slowly convincing the church members my father was a degenerate sinner needing church discipline. He met with members individually, gaining their trust and respect. Planting thoughts of my father's weaknesses in their heads, he asked questions like "Has John [my father] ever done anything you've questioned or made you angry or hurt you?" When they answered no, he persisted by asking, "Are you sure? Now, really think back. Has there ever been a time . . . ?"

He used these same tactics—gaslighting, and the power of suggestion—on me for years. The church members began recalling my father's small infractions or imperfections, which my husband capitalized on by blowing them out of proportion, causing discord. Soon he instigated an inquest, and this resulted in a "witch trial," subjecting my father to all sorts of humiliation. This situation was another example of his uncanny power over people and the lengths to which he would go to gain control.

THIS SITUATION WAS ANOTHER EXAMPLE OF HIS UNCANNY POWER OVER PEOPLE AND THE LENGTHS TO WHICH HE WOULD GO TO GAIN CONTROL.

Out of fear of losing me and my sons and to avoid further damage to the church, my father submitted. My husband forced him into a stranglehold, as he did me. Knowing how I loved and respected my parents, he wanted to disgrace them in front of me and the church to exalt himself. When I recall my father's pitiful state, my heart breaks.

We stayed in San Antonio a while longer under these very strained conditions, and this culminated with my husband reviling my mother and accusing her of an array of transgressions. Unknown to my husband, a church member was in my parents' home at the time and heard his tirade. When he realized the conversation had been overheard, he abruptly decided to leave San Antonio and move back to Louisiana where he started his own small church consisting of his parents and a few loyal friends. Born of egotistical and self-righteous motives, the church was unsustainable and soon disbanded.

Hoping for Better Days

After a year and a half in Louisiana, as the church he started began to disintegrate, my husband was invited to be associate minister at a rather large church in California. In retrospect, I realize no church, including this one, ever fully investigated my husband's past dealings with churches—a mistake for which they all paid a high price. I became so accustomed to enabling and hiding that I didn't attempt to expose him. However, every invitation to another church sparked hope that the situation would improve and my husband would finally become accountable and change his ways. This time, I hoped our wilderness time in Louisiana was over and better times were on the horizon. A large congregation meeting in a beautiful new facility, this church was strong and had well-established leadership.

I loved California. Receiving a salary on which we could live comfortably for the first time, we resided in a lovely neighborhood; I began to truly feel at home. It was also the first time in our marriage that I began forming close female friendships—not close enough to risk exposing the abuse, but close enough to consider some of them my dearest friends even to this day. My sons, who were nine and four when we moved there, also developed friendships, giving them some sense of normalcy. These circumstances provided me a much-needed sense of security and endeared California to my heart.

Despite all the good, my sons and I were nonetheless still forced to endure the bad. One night, after a few days of brooding, my husband came in carrying his briefcase as if he were protecting it. Now thirteen years into the marriage, I had dealt frequently with my husband's addiction to pornography and had become quite familiar with his patterns. My suspicions that he was hiding pornography in the briefcase were correct. Feeling cornered by my questioning, he began screaming, throwing furniture, and breaking objects; then he stormed out of the house. After he left, I found John lying in the dark, weeping in fear. We lay on the living room floor until he finally fell asleep while I hugged him and reassured him. It broke my heart to see my son so emotionally distraught.

This scenario was not an isolated event. I remember another time lying on the bedroom floor—one son on each side of me—while I told them funny stories from my childhood in an effort to dispel their fears stemming from my husband's tirade. Concerned about what abuse could do to my sons, I desired to shield them—but I couldn't. Instead, I did my best to pick up the pieces of their broken hearts after each disturbing episode.

My husband's pornographic addictions escalated during our time in California. I was shocked to find that, during one of his disappearances, he'd gone to a strip club. I was sickened with feelings of horror and betrayal. As I tried to process my emotions, my husband acted as if this wasn't a big deal, that he expected me to just "get over it." I remember turning to the Bible for comfort and coming across this verse in the Psalms: "He heals the brokenhearted and binds up their wounds" (147:3). Since my husband was anything but sympathetic to my feelings, the verse was a comfort during an extremely difficult time. Until then I had been unaware of his visits to strip clubs. Over time, I learned they were more frequent than I realized.

We stayed in central California for three years. Amazingly, and even with the extreme difficulties, I still consider those years to be the best of our marriage. However, my husband abruptly departed the church after the elders began challenging his pursuit of authority and when he jeopardized his relationship with his one true ally, the church's pulpit minister. A short time later we moved away. Leaving my close friendships and the one place I felt at home was extremely difficult. In my mind we were taking a huge step backward. Once again we returned to Louisiana, and once again I was in despair. As we left California, I felt my sense of security slipping away.

Escalated Abuse

One morning during our move from California to Louisiana, my sons and I awoke in our hotel to bear the brunt of rage the likes of which we rarely saw. With my husband sullen and abrasive, I felt the tensions building and knew at any moment the dam could break. The outburst was so unsettling I didn't recover for months.

While spending a few days in Arizona we planned to visit a church one Sunday morning. My sons and I waited in the car while my husband, running late as usual, angrily slammed the car door and began blaming me for his being late—though he'd stayed in bed until the last minute. Such psychological projection is typical with narcissistic abusers; they believe they are never at fault and everyone else is to blame. I started the car and began what I knew would be a precarious ride to church.

Soon my husband's scolding turned into yelling with his behavior spiraling out of control. In one of my rare moments of standing up to him, I indignantly exclaimed we were not at fault.

IN ONE OF MY RARE MOMENTS OF STANDING UP TO HIM, I INDIGNANTLY EXCLAIMED WE WERE NOT AT FAULT. GETTING OUT OF THE CAR, I REBELLIOUSLY ANNOUNCED, "I AM GOING TO WALK TO CHURCH TO WORSHIP MY LORD!"

Getting out of the car, I rebelliously announced, "I am going to walk to church to worship my Lord!" He drove the car beside me, demanding that I get back inside. I continued to object, but finally complied. As I started getting back in, he grabbed my arm and yanked me into the car, ripping my dress from the neck to the waist. Jerking me back and forth by my arm like a rag doll, his fingers felt as if they were pressing through bone. He then grasped my face so hard I could feel the inside of my cheek crushing against my teeth. My sons, now 12 and 7, were traumatized. While Seth whimpered in fear, John pleaded with his dad to stop. My husband threateningly chided John in "tough guy" language: "Oh! You a big man! You gonna stand up like a man for your mama?!" Realizing his pleas were useless, John sat quietly as his father continued his maniacal ranting.

Suddenly my husband threw the car in drive and headed for the church. Devastated by what had just occurred and unsure how I could face the church members—especially with my dress shredded down the front—I didn't argue. When we got out of the car, my husband commanded Seth to walk on the other side of him and opposite me. Terrified because of what he had witnessed, Seth wanted to be near me for comfort and protection but quietly obeyed his father; he was still whimpering. My husband was punishing me by punishing Seth, as he'd done many times before. His punishment extended to forcing us to walk into church in our emotionally battered state.

As we entered the building, people were nearby to greet us. In a stupor, I tried my best to smile and happily respond to their greetings. A continual flow of people welcomed us as if we were celebrities; my stomach was churning as I tried to process the morning's events. The church was small and awkwardly quiet. Abruptly, my husband loudly requested, "Could you all please let us alone and allow us to worship in peace?" Mortified, I think I blacked out for a second or two. I wanted to die—or at least vanish. The sweet people politely followed his bizarre request and left us alone, although I was certain everyone noticed my torn dress along with Seth's tears and realized something awful had just occurred. Nauseous throughout the service, I couldn't wait to leave although the church members were nothing but kind and welcoming.

After what seemed like an eternity, we finally left the church and traveled an hour to a hotel. When we got to our room my husband immediately climbed into bed and pulled the covers over his head; this signaled he would not be communicating for a long time. Emotionally exhausted, I fell into bed but slept fitfully.

The next morning while my husband remained silent and sullen under a blanket, I took the boys to Oak Creek Canyon to play near the river in hopes of providing relief from the stress. Because the hotel room was dark, I didn't notice the bruising on my face, neck, and arms. However, the boys did, and they asked me about it. Seeing their concerned expressions, I implied it wasn't a big deal, that I just bruised easily. I don't think they bought my explanation, but they dropped the subject. I did my best to help them enjoy the day together—laughing and playing—while still reeling inside from the emotional trauma of the previous day.

When we returned to the hotel, my husband had miraculously recovered from his dark mood. If true to form, his "recovery" simply indicated he'd gotten his porn fix. He "apologized" for hurting me, and I acted as if everything was fine.

He spent the next few days being attentive and happily engaged in family activities.

Disturbed by the realization of the escalation of physical abuse, I mentally replayed the incident for months. Unable to reveal the abuse to anyone, I picked myself up and continued with life as though things were normal. Likewise, I knew my sons would never expose the secret, for they too were silent victims and becoming masters at the charade of all of us being the model family. Never fully recovering from the trauma until I left the marriage, I increasingly retreated into the shell of my secret existence. I never expected that we would be free.

Does Anyone Care?

We left California in 1998. I stayed in the shambles of this marriage another fifteen years, moving from state to state and church to church. During those years the abuse continued; there were too many incidents to recount. It stole every part of who I was. However, one particular display of his insanity stands out.

One beautiful day in 2003, while I was driving down the interstate, my husband asked me a simple question, supposedly wanting my opinion on a decision he needed to make. When I did not give him the answer he wanted, he began punching the dash and screaming at me while banging the back of his head against the headrest. Next, he thrust his body out the window as far as his abdomen, screaming like a demonized woman and waving his arms wildly. Because of the spectacle I was witnessing, I was stunned and struggled to keep my eyes on the road.

Suddenly I saw the flashing lights of a sheriff's vehicle and pulled over to the side of the road. Instantly snapping out of his rage, my husband sat back in the car, calm and collected. An officer approached the passenger window and inquired, "Is there a problem?" Acting as if we were out for a Sunday drive, my husband turned on his charm, offering a manipulative and deceptive response. I was stunned at how easily the officer accepted my husband's explanation. Seemingly unconcerned, he let us go with no consequences. How could we be so easily dismissed given the exhibition the officer had witnessed? The officer's passive response was concerning. It revealed how little awareness people have about abuse and confirmed how often they miss warning signs—evidence of how much work is needed to raise awareness about this subject.

More Victimization

For the sake of clarifying what victimization looks like, and to provide insight into the daily life of a victim, I want to provide a quick snapshot into a few more of my experiences: my ex-husband broke windshields, punched holes in walls, tore doors off hinges, threw furniture. He destroyed possessions having great meaning and sentimental value to me. For example, as an anniversary gift one year he gave me an adorable stuffed bear with a heart-shaped locket around its neck, only to later completely rip it to shreds in a rage. He monitored what I ate and drank. On one occasion he smashed a cup of cappuccino against the car's console, drenching the windshield, the dash, and me; he screamed he didn't want me to drink it. He commented about my weight; one time he told me how concerned he was about how "chunky" I was getting. He screamed like a madman at his mother, driving erratically through interstate traffic while she begged him to stop because of the severe head pain and dizziness she was suffering from his screams. He has treated my daughters-in-law and granddaughter dreadfully, displaying his contempt for them and keeping them at arm's length, and he has attempted to alienate them from the family. He even abused our dogs, wrapping duct tape around our golden retriever's muzzle to prohibit him from barking, and beating our German shepherd with a railroad cross tie.

I later learned several of his behaviors were crimes, including false imprisonment, child abuse, animal cruelty, reckless driving, and sexual assault. Although my sons and I suffered for a very long time, I didn't use the word abuse until months after I had left.

After episodes of evil behavior, my sons and I were manipulated into accepting his terms of reconciliation. He would lavish us with expensive gifts such as the huge flat-screen television he bought after destroying our other one in a rage, or the truck he bought John after beating him mercilessly with a fishing rod. Tokens of his narcissistic sorrow, these gifts only increased the mind games.

In my pitiful efforts to be "enough" in a destructive and imbalanced relationship, I completely lost my identity. I grew to expect nothing to benefit me as I morphed into what he wanted me to be. Because of his spiritual abuse, I jeopardized what

I WAS CONDITIONED NOT TO FEEL, NOT TO THINK FOR MYSELF, NOT TO SHOW EMOTION, NOT TO MAKE DECISIONS, NOT TO QUESTION, NOT TO FORM MY OWN BELIEF SYSTEM. A BRAIN-WASHED ROBOT, I WAS EMPTY.

was most precious to me, my relationship with Jesus Christ. I was conditioned not to feel, not to think for myself, not to show emotion, not to make decisions, not to question, not to form my own belief system. A brain-washed robot, I was empty.

Because of his unpredictable behavior I never knew what was coming next. When explosive or destructive incidents occurred in our home, I was convinced I was at fault. As punishment, my husband would pout and withhold affection or conversation or would scream, "Why do you push me to do this?!" He frequently switched topics or evaded questions to keep from appearing to be wrong or being caught in a deceit.

Compounding the problem, Satan infiltrated my desperation with the most horrible thoughts. With my need for relief so great, the death of one or both of us seemed the only way out. I would have welcomed a fatal cancer diagnosis. While driving, I would think about crashing into a tree in hopes that either he or I would die. I wanted him dead. Evidence of how sick I became in heart, mind, body, and soul, those thoughts were not indicative of my true nature, and I deeply regret them.

To function, I shifted into survival mode, and this is where the most damage was done, as I fought to avoid facing the truth. It's incredible what people will do to simply survive, and the tricks their mind will play on them in the process. Staying in the marriage until it nearly destroyed me, I believed leaving was not an option; I feared the worst if I did. I don't know how I endured such an exhausting and devastating existence for so long.

Desperation

Growing increasingly worse, the abuse cycle defined my marriage. Just when I would believe my marriage might improve, another episode emerged—each more sinister and difficult to endure. With every passing year I was less equipped to cope and more desperate for relief. Accepting the circumstances of my life was my destiny. I became overwhelmed with defeat, depression, and despair.

When my sons grew up and were out of the house, I felt I lacked purpose. Growing increasingly despondent, I spent many days in bed staring lifelessly at the TV. I had no hope and became less involved in ministerial activities. With my depression apparent to others, I kept people at arm's length and didn't share my inner feelings with anyone. Although I had people in my life I loved and who loved me, I couldn't keep the secret from exposure if I allowed

GROWING INCREASINGLY WORSE, THE ABUSE CYCLE DEFINED MY MARRIAGE. JUST WHEN I WOULD BELIEVE MY MARRIAGE MIGHT IMPROVE, ANOTHER EPISODE EMERGED— EACH MORE SINISTER AND DIFFICULT TO ENDURE.

others to get too close. Each day was a minute-by-minute struggle, and the years took their toll.

Desperate for relief, I eventually devised a plan—in 2010, twenty-seven years into my marriage—to end this nightmare. Perhaps because he'd never hit me, I still didn't recognize—or perhaps wouldn't admit—that my marriage was abusive. I simply knew my misery was influencing every aspect of my life.

Surprised at my courage to strategize an escape, I began implementing each step. Sorting and storing my belongings discreetly in the garage, I prepared to load them quickly into a vehicle and escape when the right moment came. Thanks to a friend in Arizona who owned a restaurant and a finance company, I secured two job opportunities. Without a vehicle to call my own, I planned to rent a car to get to Arizona and then use the bus system or a bicycle for transportation until I could do better. I considered former necessities luxuries I could do without. I wanted out. I planned to stay with a friend for a short time until I could get on my feet. Two hundred dollars—a Christmas gift from a family member—hidden in a secret bank account was my only financial lifeline. With all my preparations complete, I awaited my departure date.

On the day before I was scheduled to leave, I finalized putting my plan into action. To obtain the rental car secretly since the town where we lived didn't have a rental car agency, I was crafty in devising my scheme. Having checked the bus schedule to travel to a town twenty-five miles away, I arranged to rent a car. Very early, before daylight, and before my husband would be out of bed, I snuck out a window in the bedroom on the other end of the house from where he was sleeping. Walking to the nearby bus stop, I boarded a bus to the rental agency. Because my husband slept very late, I had plenty of time. In less than twenty-four hours, my misery would be over. A perfect exit scenario—like a scene out of a movie.

I was horribly anxious on the bus ride, and fear overcame me as I went through second thoughts. Nevertheless, I was determined. This was my way out, and I was going to take it. I rented a car and drove the thirty miles back home, parking away from the house to avoid alerting my husband's suspicions. I crawled back inside the house through the same window. He was still asleep in the other room, clueless I was even gone. When he left the house, my plans were to load my belongings in the rental car, keep it parked down the street, and then leave in the middle of the night. However, with a gnawing in the pit of my stomach, I sensed this decision was not right.

As my anxiety mounted, questions began swirling in my head. *What would my leaving do to my children? What would it do to the church? Who would I hurt in the process?* I don't know if it was fear, concern for other people's feelings, or the Spirit's conviction. Maybe it was guilt or self-condemnation. Perhaps it was my husband's control over me or poor timing. Perhaps it was a combination of all these factors. Regardless of the reason, questions gave way to a change of heart in a matter of minutes. I decided I couldn't leave—not this way.

Sad and disappointed, I rose long before dawn the next morning, climbed out the window once more, returned the rental car, rode the bus home, and climbed back through the window before most people were even awake. I made the choice to stay, but my resolve gave me strength for what was to come.

More than disappointed, I now felt empowered.

With my newfound determination I began striving to be a better wife and show affection to my husband, even though doing so made me nauseous. I resolved to be a better minister's wife, a better friend, more spiritual. I made every effort to make myself better and try to make my marriage work. Determined to go the distance, I exerted the little strength left in me.

I know now there was a purpose for my window escape and the following eighteen months. God always has a purpose. Looking back, I'm grateful for the lesson God's divine plan wove into my life. This experience confirmed in my heart that I left nothing off the table. All my cards were played; I gave my marriage my all. With every option exhausted, when the true, God-ordained timing for my departure became evident a year and a half later, I didn't regret the choice I was forced to make.

The Breaking Point

Everyone has a breaking point, I suppose. Mine came one cold night in the spring of 2012 when I stood shivering violently, trying to grasp what had just transpired. In the midst of the terror I experienced, I finally began stepping out of the fog in which I'd lived for so long. Though I still wasn't capable of using the word abuse, God made me realize my situation was dire.

The evening began as nothing out of the ordinary but devolved, dramatically so, into the destructive pattern to which I was accustomed. Over the years I usually remained silent when I was being verbally attacked. In the months immediately preceding this incident, however, I began finding my voice and a shred of courage. As my husband began a tirade, I decided to escape for the night. I needed time alone to think, if only for a few hours.

Surprising myself, I resolutely got into my car and sped away. With no particular destination in mind, I drove through my neighborhood thinking I had escaped. However, after traveling only a few blocks, I saw headlights in the rearview mirror—he was chasing me. Something erupted in me and made me determined I was not going to cave to his behavior. A high-speed chase ensued.

Eventually, fleeing my pursuer, I merged onto a highway with no obstacles in my path. Trying to maneuver alongside the driver's side of my vehicle, he lost control when his tire suddenly got caught in the gravel on the road's left shoulder. Swerving violently, his vehicle flipped on its side and skidded down the highway, spraying sparks like fireworks in the night sky. I watched in horror in my rearview mirror. His car finally stopped on the shoulder of the road in a crumpled mass, the wheels spinning like tops. In my distorted mind-set, my first inclination was relief, but this was instantly replaced with the overwhelming thought that the wreck was my fault and my husband might well be dead because of me.

Whimpering in terror, I turned around and drove back to his car while praying he wasn't dead. As I stepped out of my vehicle and into what felt like an out-of-body experience, I began trembling and became intensely aware of the cold and the horrific scene before me. All was eerily silent except for the whirring of the spinning tires. I somehow remained composed enough to approach his crumpled car and assess the situation.

Questions tumbled through my mind: *What will I find? Is he critically injured? Will he be dismembered? Is he dead?*

The trauma sent me into shock. He was pressed—seemingly lifeless—against the driver's side door, which was lying on the ground. He was bleeding, but I couldn't tell from where. Pounding on the broken windshield, I began screaming his name and shouting, "Are you OK?!" I was begging for a response. In retrospect, I realize his refusal to respond was a shock tactic. Finally, he began to move. Then I heard him say these words: "Are you going to leave me, baby? Please don't leave me! I love you! I love Jesus! Are you going to leave me?" His incessant ranting was like that of a madman—manipulative and controlling—even in the face of what could have been death.

Like a light switch being flipped in a dark room, I realized the degree of insanity I'd been living with for all those years—though, astoundingly, still never considering it abuse. I looked up at the moon and begged God to see me, to help me, to give me direction. In a split-second, years of questions and trauma were summarized in one query: "God, do you see?" And I heard a voice within me confirm that the answer was yes: "I have seen enough." Having no idea what those words meant or where they would lead, I knew God had embraced me in His arms, assuring me the situation was under control. In my brokenness, I trusted Him. Weeping, I allowed myself to admit, "I can't do this anymore."

I LOOKED UP AT THE MOON AND BEGGED GOD TO SEE ME, TO HELP ME, TO GIVE ME DIRECTION.

Eventually, emergency medical personnel and police arrived at the scene and began assessing the situation. After much resistance and at the officers' insistence, my husband reluctantly agreed to go to the emergency room. Watching him being loaded onto a gurney and into an ambulance, I sat shivering in shock on the side of the highway. The emergency workers quizzed me to evaluate my mental state: "What is your name?" "How old are you?" "Where do you live?" "Do you know what day it is?" Abruptly, one of the officers asked a question that unnerved me: "Was there domestic violence involved in this crash?" "No!" I emphatically insisted while contemplating what the officer would think about what had just occurred. From somewhere deep inside, I doubted my response, and I think he did too.

In that moment, vocalizing the word abuse was not an option for me. Unaware that all the years of my marriage could have been summed up in one word, I didn't know my experiences had a name. (After all, he never hit me.) But now, somehow, despite my ignorance, reality began unfolding. All the hiding, all the rationalizing, all the enabling led me to this moment. Lights began flashing in my mind and past traumas came into focus as though I was waking from a dream. Although I wasn't fully aware of the magnitude of it all, my dark secret was beginning to be revealed—even to me.

> UNAWARE THAT ALL THE YEARS OF MY MARRIAGE COULD HAVE BEEN SUMMED UP IN ONE WORD, I DIDN'T KNOW MY EXPERIENCES HAD A NAME.

Meanwhile, the night turned even more bizarre. When I entered the emergency room, my husband was standing in his hospital gown, his arm bandaged. He looked at me and made one of the most ludicrous comments I ever heard him utter:

"I just realized we never got to dance together." Hugging me close, he began swaying—a maneuver to keep me under his spell. As the room began spinning, I felt faint and thought I would vomit. As he climbed back in bed, I stood there with tears streaming down my face, broken in every way. Then he patted my hand and said something I translated as "It's OK. We know this is your fault, but I'm going to be fine."

The following days were filled with many dramatic scenarios, too many to describe. Thankfully, the only physical injury my husband suffered was to his arm, and it healed quickly. As for me, those days became a blur as I was plagued with post-traumatic, stress-induced mental and physical health issues. Having already made plans to go to Texas to visit my parents a couple of weeks later, I decided I would tell them everything and expose what I had worked to hide all those years. During those two weeks before my trip, I prayed constantly: "God, for the first time, I'm worried about myself. I feel I am on the verge of a breakdown. Help me hold on—just until I get home. Just help me to get home."

Gratefulness filled my heart each night as I realized I had made it through one more day. Ultimately, He sustained me, giving me strength and courage as I navigated the terrifying process of deciding to at least temporarily leave my dysfunctional marriage.

Child Abuse

"Fathers, do not exasperate your children; instead, bring them up in the training and instruction of the Lord" (Ephesians 6:4).

Abuse and My Children

Domestic abuse adversely affects the whole family, especially the children. When thinking about writing this chapter, I recoil—both physically and mentally. I don't want to revisit the horrors or invoke the images pressing my heart against the edge of a sword causing me to bleed profusely from the wound. Hyperventilating as I sit at my computer, I know the labyrinth of pain I will be exposing as I write about what my children—especially John, my firstborn—suffered by being thrust into a world of abuse.

There are some things I can't forget, images I can't "unsee," behaviors I will never understand, regrets that still haunt me. Satan whispers to remind me what I did wrong, what I could have done differently, what I should have done, what I should have changed. The anguish of knowing I was an unwilling party to my children's abuse could allow Satan to have the upper hand. But I have forgiven myself, and I know God has forgiven me. The road to forgiveness, however, has not been without pain, nor my failures without cost. I am inexpressibly sorry for those failures. Therefore, despite my regrets, detailing this part of my story is necessary to hopefully spare other women and children horrific pain.

The Subject of Children

In the beginning of my marriage, I should have known the subject of having children would be a sensitive one. During our engagement my soon-to-be husband sent me a twenty-page letter explaining why children were not a priority. The letter detailed how he believed he'd been prepared by God to jet across the world proclaiming His message to stadiums overflowing with people—he believed he would live out a sort of self-acclaimed Billy Graham scenario. He described his accolades in sports, how much he sacrificed by giving up past girlfriends, and the suffering he endured to serve God. Reflecting his arrogance and self-absorption, the letter suggested children would be an inconvenience.

A year or so into our marriage, while we were at a restaurant, the subject of children arose, and it included the discussion of how long we should wait before having them. I commented on his age being a consideration since he was 31. Although I was merely stating a fact, he was offended. He yelled and pounded the table, nearly turning it over, and threw food everywhere—especially on me. He stormed out of the restaurant and left me to walk out alone with everyone staring. I was mortified. He made his point, and I never alluded to his age or discussed children again—unless he did.

However, a couple of years later, he announced we could start trying to have children. Looking back, his announcement came across as though he were doing me a favor. Regardless, I was happy and hoped his becoming a father would change him for the better. I was wrong.

Pregnancy

After being married three years, I became pregnant with our first child. While we were visiting my grandparents, I took a home pregnancy test one morning, and this confirmed my suspicions. Having a child was the most glorious experience I could imagine; I was ecstatic and couldn't wait to tell my husband. From the time I was a little girl, I had dreamed of this moment. His response, however, shattered my dream. Forcing a smile, emotionless, he responded, "That's great." I was crushed. Unfortunately, his reaction to my pregnancy was a sign of things to come.

He abruptly left my grandparents' house without indicating where he was going or when he would be back. He didn't return until very late at night. I suppose he needed to go pout about a baby being in the picture, that he would no longer be the center of my universe. His place would now have to be shared, inconveniencing his schedule and threatening his sovereignty.

The eight-hour trip home from my grandparents' house a few days later was drama-filled. Barely speaking until about halfway home, he suddenly began yelling and accusing me of being unaffectionate and inattentive. Wanting the rant to stop, I apologized even though his accusations were false. Disappointed about my pregnancy, he was punishing me. Truthfully, I think he wanted me to apologize for being pregnant. When we got home, he mysteriously vanished for two days. Quite sick at this point in the pregnancy, I didn't care.

Despite the stress in my life, I knew the necessity of taking care of myself physically and emotionally. SpaghettiOs were my best friend in more ways than one during those days. Being the only food I could eat which eased the nausea, this canned food somehow comforted my lonely soul. I went to all my doctor and sonogram appointments alone, and my husband seemed unconcerned about them. In the joy of expecting my baby, his disinterest didn't deter me from doing all I could to keep my baby and myself healthy.

Throughout the pregnancy my husband expressed his disapproval. More than once he emphasized how my role wouldn't change just because I was pregnant. One evening when my mom came to visit us in Louisiana, we all went to visit my in-laws. My tummy was very large, and getting up from a seated position was difficult. I made the mistake of asking him to bring me a glass of water when he came to the living room from the kitchen. He emphatically announced he was not my servant and my request was inappropriate. Both of our mothers were shocked and expressed their concern over his behavior, but their reprimands fell on deaf ears.

A few months later, after moving to Texas, I was diagnosed with prenatal toxemia. Horribly swollen, with my blood pressure at a dangerous level, I was confined to total bed rest.

> BEGGING HIM TO ACKNOWLEDGE MY FEAR, I FOOLISHLY TOOK RESPONSIBILITY FOR HIS ACTIONS— THE CLASSIC VICTIM'S RESPONSE.

Thankfully, my parents lived only two hours away, so I stayed with them during the last few weeks of my pregnancy. I was grateful for the reprieve from my turbulent homelife. However, one night after awaking about 2 a.m. from a terrifying dream about the abuse I suffered, I wrote my husband a long letter telling him about the dream. Unfortunately, by the third page, the letter morphed into my apology for anything I did to prompt his abusive behavior. Begging him to acknowledge my fear, I foolishly took responsibility for his actions—the classic victim's response. Prompted by constant turmoil and fear, the dream was a revelation of my pitiful state of mind.

John's Birth

Just after we moved to Texas for our first full-time ministry position, my first son John was born six weeks premature. Excited and scared, I left for the hospital early one morning. After serious complications from toxemia, I gave birth later in the day. Although my condition was touch and go for a couple of days, God miraculously brought me through. Temporarily rising to the occasion, my husband showed concern during this crisis. This proved the complexity of his character.

Adjusting to life with an infant was difficult. I was awakened almost every half-hour through the night, and my days consisted of a constant barrage of infant screams. I believe John sensed the stress in our home and was afraid and insecure. During John's infancy I received almost no help from my husband. Not to be burdened with tasks like helping with housework or being part of his infant son's care, he never helped with meals or errands, he never got up with John, never rocked him, never comforted him. I'm not sure he changed one diaper. A single parent in many ways, I was overwhelmed.

On Sundays I arose after little sleep and got John and myself ready for church. Packing the diaper bag and grabbing my purse, my Bible, and the baby, I tried to be in the car on time to avoid getting in trouble. Most of the time my husband preferred I drive to church and let him out at the door, park the car, and gather the baby and my belongings before scrambling up to the second row of the sanctuary in full view of everyone.

He believed these tasks were my job, and his job was the much more important one, with eternal souls at stake. On potluck Sundays I made two trips to the car and back because my husband wouldn't even carry in a casserole dish. In short, going to church on Sundays was an ordeal.

John's Victimization

Emotionally distant from John from the time he was born, my husband seemed incapable of being a loving father. I tried not to believe he cared so little about his son. His lack of emotional attachment prompted shocking behavior. One day, angry because we made plans to visit my parents in a nearby city, screaming how tired he was, my husband violently grabbed my two-month-old son out of my arms and held him in the palm of one hand at arm's length with no support underneath. Dangling in midair, John began screaming. I repeatedly tried to rescue him, but my husband would jerk him out of my reach, yelling I was not going to get the baby back. Overwhelmed with maternal instinct as I listened to my baby scream while his father acted like a madman, I defaulted to my usual recourse: apologizing until my husband calmed down. When he finally gave John back to me, we left for my parents' house. During the silent two-hour ride, I was heartbroken and physically ill as I wondered how he could mistreat his infant son.

Unfortunately, the mistreatment continued through the years.

Overbearing and aloof, my husband took pleasure in intimidating John. When John was about two, I watched my husband force him to view animated and roaring lifelike dinosaurs at a museum, holding him tightly and threatening him if he cried. About the same time, my husband attempted to teach him some math when John was playing with pennies. When John couldn't grasp the concept at such a young age, my husband began yelling and berating him. The incident ended with John sobbing while his dad continued his tirade, throwing pennies on the floor for John to count until finally tiring of the spectacle.

On Christmas Day 1989, two-year-old John was thrilled when he received a motorized red shiny jeep from my in-laws. Still a small boy, he struggled with learning to drive it. Attempting to quickly train him to use the pedals and steering wheel, my husband chased John around the yard, screaming at him to apply the brakes. Overtaken by his nerves, John nearly ran into a tree. Violently jerking his son out of the jeep by his arms, my husband held John to his face, screaming. The mental picture of John sobbing and his little legs dangling while his dad seethed and spit in his face still brings me to tears. More distressing was that my in-laws and I stood there watching and did nothing. Three adults did not attempt to rescue John, nor did we say a word—evidence of my husband's control over all of us. The shiny red jeep lost its luster, and John seldom rode in it again.

THIS PATTERN CONTINUED, AND I ANGUISHED OVER THE THOUGHT OF REJECTION'S POTENTIAL IMPACT. JOHN COULD NEVER WIN THE APPROVAL OR AFFECTION OF HIS FATHER.

When John was four, he proudly ran into the room

one day to reveal a drawing he had painstakingly completed. When my husband saw it, he scoffed, offering no words of confirmation or encouragement, communicating that he thought John's effort was foolish. John's face dropped in crushing disappointment.

This pattern continued, and I anguished over the thought of rejection's potential impact. John could never win the approval or affection of his father, who thought his son could never be enough nor ever do anything right. In fact, my husband's abusive behavior toward John continues to the time of my writing this book.

John's Ongoing Abuse

In the early '70s, my husband was an Olympic hopeful, fueling his narcissism and later intensifying the pressure he put on our sons to excel in every area of life. Outstanding performances were a matter of image through which he could receive recognition. So whether in sports, academics, or biblical knowledge, our sons' most notable accomplishments were, according to my husband, a reflection of his training. His counterfeit image as the ideal father and instructor had to be maintained at any price.

When John was small my husband began drilling him in learning Bible verses and even the Greek alphabet because, after all, a two-year-old needs to know Greek for proper biblical interpretation. If he didn't perform well, John was either berated and threatened or punished. Always fearing the worst, I dreaded the nights he would call John into our bedroom for his Greek lesson and Scripture memorization. Some nights ended pleasantly, but many ended with John in tears.

John became a conduit for my husband to project his image as an amazing and spiritually discerning father. Frequently forcing John to perform on videos, my husband insisted the songs be sung correctly, the Scripture quoted perfectly, or the Bible story told flawlessly.

Sickened by the memories surrounding those videos, I can't watch them. A bundle of nerves, John was afraid he might miss the mark. With no one outside our home knowing what went on behind the scenes, my husband's image remained intact.

When John was three, my husband made John "preach" one Sunday. Wearing a tiny red bow tie and standing on a chair behind a pulpit, John delivered a message that would have been difficult for the most seasoned biblical orator. Looking small and overwhelmed, John would fearfully glance over to get his father's approval; if he made a mistake, fear would be etched on his little face. However, the "show" was adorable to many, and thus it successfully boosted my husband's ego.

Enabling him to boast about how he had instilled the Bible in one so young, John was exploited for my husband's own benefit.

My husband also involved our young sons in competitive sports, another self-serving pursuit. I believe he thought he could live vicariously through their accomplishments. Although I loved the idea of my sons being good athletes, I hated the performance pressure my husband imposed on them.

When John was about four, my husband started teaching him to high jump. I came home one day to find them practicing in the yard. When John looked at me for approval, I proudly responded, "That's great, John!" Indicative of the misery I was certain John endured while I was gone, my husband angrily responded, "No, it's not! He's not doing it right!" John's little face grew more worried with every attempt he made to jump; he knew things would not end well.

Another practice session ended traumatically when John was out with his father one day. When John couldn't complete a jump, my husband beat the measuring pole on top of the car, screamed liked a crazed man in John's face, and yanked him in the air by his jeans so forcefully they were nearly ripped off his body. My husband purchased new jeans before they got home and instructed John not to tell me about the incident—a secret he kept until he was an adult. When I think of John keeping his secret and suffering the trauma alone, my heart breaks.

These athletic "workout" sessions continued as John grew up, and Seth joined in when he was old enough. When my husband would tell the boys it was time to go "work out," I could see their anxious expressions. Unfortunately, Seth was a captive audience of the horrible treatment of his brother, and sometimes he would tell me about it. Most of the time, however, he knew not to say anything. One time, a dear friend of ours—an older gentleman—went with my husband and boys for one of these workout sessions. Returning later with a concerned look on his face, he expressed his worries about John based on what he'd witnessed. As always, I felt helpless to stop the mistreatment.

The sport John was most involved in and passionate about was baseball, and I loved going to his games; those remain a precious memory to this day. Sometimes, however, the games were extremely stressful because John would not be playing to my husband's expectations. Expressing his disappointment, his father called out corrections to John from the stands. John and I knew miserable discussions would follow, or the workouts would be extremely difficult the next day. One night when John was a young boy, we returned from a game in which he didn't maneuver out of the batter's box quickly enough to avoid being struck by a pitch. When we returned home, my husband forced John to stand in front of the garage door while he forcefully hurled baseballs at him, yelling at him to move. Hearing the baseballs pound the garage door, I was incredibly anxious; they practiced in the dark using only the car's headlights for lighting. Despite the danger of these drills, thankfully John wasn't injured. However, no matter the outcome, this ludicrous scenario was just another way my husband instilled fear in his son.

With punishments becoming more extreme as he got older, the belittling and the daily pressure for John to please his father were incessant. The more pressure he experienced, the more concerned I became about the long-term effects. With my fears mounting as the abuse became more severe, I felt helpless. When John was about seven, he innocently laughed about something my husband thought was inappropriate. As a result, our plans with family at an amusement park were disrupted. John was forced to stay behind with his father. Although I begged to stay home, my husband refused my request. I was horrified when I returned in the evening to a sickening sight. My brother, who stopped by, pointed to John and said, "Look at his legs!" I couldn't believe my eyes. Dark blue and deep purple bruises and red welts covered John from just above his buttocks down to his ankles. Proudly describing how he taught John a lesson by whipping him with a small tree limb, my husband instructed me to ensure John wore long pants for the next few weeks to hide the bruises—all this indicated his awareness of the beating's severity. Even now I'm horrified at the thought of it all. Despite how much I objected, I could do nothing.

As time passed, the punishments became increasingly perverse. One cold night my husband made John sleep in the woods in a snake-infested shed with only a roof and one wall for protection—as though he were unworthy to sleep under the same roof as his family when he displeased his father. This incident happened just after my husband beat John with a fishing rod, demanding him to cry, as if crying would end the beating. Because I couldn't stand to see and hear John's agony, I left the house. Apart from pleading, once again I did nothing to stop this abuse. Foolishly, I accepted my husband's quoting of Proverbs 23:12: "If you beat your son with a rod, he will not die." He believed this verse validated this kind of mistreatment of his son.

Despite all the abuse, John was always respectful when interacting with his father. One day when John was a junior in high school, he asked if he could go to a friend's house. My husband's unfounded, irate response escalated into challenging John to a fistfight to prove who was stronger. In his rage, my husband tackled John, who would not retaliate or stoop to his father's threats. My husband, on the other hand, was like a seething animal uncontrollably pouncing on its prey. Even when they toppled down a hill next to our house, John didn't fight back or resist. Knowing this degrading and foolish treatment was hard to endure, I was so proud of him for maintaining his dignity.

A few years later, when John met his future wife, the struggle for approval continued. Never fully accepting her, just as he never accepted John, my husband treated her with an aloofness, and disrespect; the details are too twisted to recount. Even more troublesome, he has treated his grand-daughter in the same way. Barely knowing either of them and never seeing them anymore, he doesn't seem to care; although they are better off not having him in their life, I am bewildered and wonder how he lives with himself. Not having those relationships is truly his loss. I pity him. He is missing some of the most precious gifts he could know, just as he missed all he could have shared with his firstborn son.

John's Depression

John was one of the most beautiful children imaginable. He had adorable curly hair, big brown eyes, brown skin, and apple cheeks. A happy, spunky, outgoing child, he embraced life with smiles and laughter, excited to see what each day would hold. Unfortunately, in the dark days of his early childhood, the sparkle slowly began to fade, and by the time he was five or six it almost disappeared because of his mental, physical, and emotional anguish. He didn't smile much anymore. One time my husband even corrected him for the way he smiled—ridiculing him during a family photo. Worn down by the pressure to perform and the constant struggle to gain his father's approval, the outgoing and cheery child I knew slowly retreated into a shell.

Sadly, John grew even more withdrawn during his teenage years as the futile struggle to please his father stole his God-given identity and was replaced with a sense of "less than" and "not enough." Blinded by ego and selfishness, his father continued the abusive behavior. For example, when John developed acne (as nearly all teenagers do), his father degraded him, chiding him about how bad it looked and accusing him of not washing his face properly.

Having struggled with depression, anxiety, and PTSD, in a recent discussion John commented on his experiences with his father: "I've been thinking, and I realized something: No matter what I accomplish or how successful I am or how I try to improve myself, I think to myself, 'Will this be enough?' But I know it won't be. Because I know now it's not about doing or being enough to get my dad's approval. The fact is he doesn't approve I even exist." Those words were heartrending to me.

Behind closed doors and behind the façade of the "perfect" family image, John's suffering resulted in long-lasting effects.

John's Victory

Fortunately, John has courageously battled to become whole again. Walking with Jesus and free of the destructive relationship with his father, John is successful and has a beautiful family. Having never gained his father's approval, and because of his father's toxic nature, John has no contact with him—a situation which is for the best, at least until his father drastically changes.

Over the years, God has created victory out of what would have spiritually destroyed some people, causing them to reject anything associated with Christianity. John has found his God-given identity in the redeeming grace of a mighty Savior. Living victoriously—free from the past and the chains binding him—John's redemption is beautiful to behold. Compassionate and extremely kindhearted—especially toward the outcast and overlooked in society—John is making a difference in the world through his generous nature and loving spirit. He lives happily and successfully with his loving wife and daughter.

Seth's Birth

From the moment I became pregnant with my younger son, Seth, my husband's excitement and acceptance was completely different compared to my pregnancy with John. He was more attentive, more compassionate, and showed more interest. The contrast in his behavior between the pregnancies seemed strange to me, and he never wavered in his joyous reception and proud acknowledgement of his younger son.

Just hours after Seth's birth, I couldn't help but notice how my husband cherished him. The gratification was clearly defined in his facial expression and outward demeanor. I distinctly remember my husband and mother-in-law boastfully claiming how Seth looked just like my husband. Seth was a docile and easygoing infant—in sharp contrast to his older brother—and my husband proudly compared Seth's quiet nature to the humble disposition of the biblical character Moses. He never made such a comparison about John, nor had I ever seen, regarding John, the pride he displayed or the affection he showered upon Seth. There could be no doubt of my husband's admiration for his newborn second son.

Seth's Victimization

Not experiencing the type of abuse John did, Seth instead suffered from self-imposed pressure to perform as a result of watching his brother's cruel treatment. In trying to avoid such treatment, he was tortured by his own pursuit of perfection in sports, social circles, academics, and life in general. Seth was never satisfied unless he excelled, or at least attempted to excel, in everything he tried. Although the extreme pressure would have broken many people, he managed it stoically for most of his early life. Seth perceived even small feats—like spinning a basketball on his finger, learning to lasso with a rope, or winning a board game—as challenges which had to be mastered.

My husband perceived Seth's accolades as feathers in his own cap. Seeking recognition for raising such a brilliant and talented son, he used every opportunity to promote Seth, thereby promoting himself. More subtle than blatant mistreatment, this form of abuse was cruel nevertheless.

In a powerful but covert attempt to maintain control, my husband groomed Seth by showering him with affection and compliments, creating an unhealthy bond between them. Seth became an obvious casualty of Stockholm Syndrome— just as his brother and I were. Capitalizing on every opportunity to portray himself as an impressive father and thereby fostering an unhealthy bond between Seth and himself, my husband even coerced Seth into signing a statement indicating he would be under his father's rule until he was 25, citing examples of biblical father-son relationships like that of Jacob and Joseph. Such an expectation clearly showed how much my husband wanted control. Although Seth signed the absurd agreement when he was young, he broke away from it when he grew older and became aware of its damaging nature.

My husband jealously guarded his dysfunctional relationship with his youngest son. Outside influences could not be allowed to interfere with the total control he desired. For example, he would take Seth away by himself—sometimes to other cities—during family gatherings to protect the exclusivity of their relationship. In addition, perceiving my father as a threat to his relationship with Seth, my husband was relentless in his attempts to belittle my father in our eyes, to characterize him as a bad guy, and to one-up him any way he could.

Honoring his tradition of purchasing all of his grandsons their first vehicle, my father found a treasured car Seth aspired to own one day. Buying a classic 1978 silver Pace Car Edition Corvette when Seth was 12, my father kept it in a garage until Seth got his driver's license.

Complaining it was old and would constantly need repairs, my husband was negative from the moment Seth received the car. Seth had barely driven it when, out of the blue, my husband sold it, claiming it was too expensive to keep. In an effort to outdo my father, he then bought Seth a brand-new Chevy Avalanche, which we couldn't afford and which my husband relinquished to the bank when he filed for bankruptcy about a year later. In fact, his need to come out on top ultimately led to his financial ruin. If the money for the Avalanche payments had been used to restore the Corvette, Seth would have owned a show-quality car, but it also would have represented a threat to my husband's control over Seth. Not to be outdone—even by a vehicle—my husband would go to any lengths to maintain control.

With status quo being inadequate for him, and in coming to terms with his burdensome relationship with his father, Seth eventually began to break under the pressure. Just after graduating from high school, Seth started to cry while trying to describe to me how he felt. His dad was pressuring him using guilt and manipulation to do a certain action he didn't want to do. It was fairly simple, but something he was being coerced to do nonetheless. Seeing a change in his personality, I was heartbroken. Seth's never-ending quest to fulfill his father's expectations of being the "golden boy" was taking its toll, as was the smothering relationship with his father.

The Good Son

In his father's emotional stranglehold, Seth felt the constant pressure of being treated as the "better son," the one "more loved." Once when our entire family—including John—was at a restaurant during the Christmas holidays, my husband made a grand production of distributing to each family member a book he had written—a memoir of sorts—identifying all of Seth's accolades and exploiting his son's obedient nature and endearing personality as proof of raising such a fine son. While implying Seth was the "good son," my husband was figuratively slapping John in the face, emphasizing my husband's unfavorable regard for him. Loving his brother deeply, Seth was shocked and humiliated. It could be clearly seen that evening in his strained facial expression.

My husband's displays of favoring Seth extended beyond the sphere of family members. On a wall of shelves in his church office in California, my husband proudly displayed trophies, awards, baseball gloves, medals, certificates, and pictures of his "golden boy." He deemed it "Seth's wall." Since by this time both boys were grown and had left home, Seth was the only son with whom church members were acquainted because of that wall. One day a man from the church overheard a conversation about John and said, "Oh, I didn't know you have another son." His response spoke volumes.

Thankfully, despite the way their father compared them, my sons have always been extremely close. Although always the underdog in my husband's eyes, John loved and was extremely protective of his younger brother. Helping to train Seth in sports, taking him fishing, and playing stickball with him in the backyard, John was the ideal brother, one Seth adored. Laughing and fighting as brothers do, they kept each other sane in the midst of the chaos. They were truly one another's keeper.

Leaving an abusive situation brings clarity. When I left the marriage and the complete picture of past experiences unfolded, Seth was overcome with guilt and called me one day, crying. "I can't believe John doesn't hate me for the way Daddy compared us," he said. Fortunately, John knew the comparisons weren't Seth's fault. Through my research and by walking alongside other abuse victims in their journeys, I've discovered abusers often have a "favorite" child, as well as a "scapegoat" child (usually the eldest) on whom they unleash their twisted disdain.

Seth eventually received counseling from and was mentored by some extraordinary men—pillars of faith, really—who were friends and father figures. All of them helped Seth process the abuse he experienced and become emotionally and spiritually healthy. From this he has been instrumental in helping others both overcome difficult circumstances and embrace the abundance afforded by a meaningful relationship with God. Now having a deeper understanding of his heavenly Father, Seth has become a spiritual mentor and an example of God's redemptive love.

Our Healing

In His incredible mercy and goodness, God powerfully healed and restored my sons and me. Although we are on separate journeys, the common thread of abuse is woven into our fiber. Nevertheless we have experienced the victory of emerging out of the darkness and into the light while choosing to live and love abundantly. Taking stock of and coming to terms with what we endured was part of the healing process for all of us.

I adore both my sons. I would marry their father all over again just for the privilege of having them. They, their wives, my granddaughter, and future grandchildren are a tremendous source of strength for me; my heart overflows with love for all of them. I don't know what I would do without them. My prayer is I will leave a legacy of love, courage, and victory for all of them because I dwell in the shadow of the cross of Christ and in the glorious presence of a resurrected Savior. I also pray we can make a difference in this world through all of our healing.

Sexual Abuse

"Marriage should be honored by all, and the marriage bed kept pure, for God will judge the adulterer and all the sexually immoral" (Hebrews 13:4).

Sexual Pressure

Although I have always been extremely uncomfortable discussing the subject of sex, I must address sexual abuse in Christian marriage. God intended sex for the benefit of both people in marriage. However, in an abusive marriage, many times the abuser is sexually gratified while the victim is left feeling degraded, invaded, and emotionally raped. Granted, sex involves exploration and spicing things up. However, when exploration becomes sexual favors rendered in response to intimidation and coercion, it becomes twisted and sick.

WHEN EXPLORATION BECOMES SEXUAL FAVORS RENDERED IN RESPONSE TO INTIMIDATION AND COERCION, IT BECOMES TWISTED AND SICK.

In a distorted effort to fulfill his selfish desires, at times my husband pressured me into sexual activities against my will, my judgment, and my conscience. As my resistance weakened, I was unaware this pressure was a form of *sexual assault*—intentionally coercing me sexually through intimidation, fear, and manipulation to engage in acts against my will. A source of humiliation and shame, sex left me feeling like a whore. Often feeling physically sick after a sexual encounter with him, I would remain still until the nausea subsided.

Looking back, I realize the sexual abuse began before my husband and I were married. I've struggled with that reality because I was, nevertheless, a willing party in my first sexual experience. However, I remember feeling and coerced and blindsided by the situation. I was a naïve 17-year-old girl with no sexual experience who succumbed to pressure from a 29-year-old man, one who, no less, was supposedly a man of God. Believing that any sexual contact outside of marriage was dangerous, immoral, and against my nature, I had successfully avoided succumbing to sex because of my father's strict rules and my own determination to stay "pure" even when situations arose tempting me to do otherwise. Somehow it was different this time, with him. I mistakenly felt protected from sexual pressure in the presence of this "godly" minister, so my guard was down. Beguiling, deceitful, he trapped me in his web before I had time to think. I remember him asking me leading questions and coaxing me into believing all would be OK. I also remember feeling I owed it to him somehow. Although the incident wasn't a full-blown sexual encounter, it was sexual in nature nonetheless. Sickened by the whole episode, I remember him intimating that it was my fault and that I should express my remorse to him. I realize now the sick nature of it all, especially considering I was underage and he was 29.

BEGUILING, DECEITFUL, HE TRAPPED ME IN HIS WEB BEFORE I HAD TIME TO THINK.

The sexual abuse continued on my wedding night. Having just turned 18, I was nervous in spite of the earlier sexual encounter. Some behaviors were not even on my radar, and I could not imagine what would be expected of me. When I refused his requests, my husband displayed his disappointment by pulling the covers around his neck, rolling over, and going to sleep. Having been married only a few hours, I already felt manipulated and sensed I was a disappointment.

After the first few days, I tried to fulfill his wishes. Thinking perhaps I was being prudish, I suppressed my shyness and hesitation and pushed through my inhibitions as I was exposed to his perverted fantasy world. Several years passed before I realized he indulged in pornography, which influenced our intimacy in devastating ways as I was sexually transformed into someone I did not recognize. On our honeymoon he presented me a beautifully wrapped box containing lingerie which would embarrass the most seasoned porn star. Humiliated and swallowing every ounce of pride, I performed my "duty." Not long after we returned from our honeymoon, I told him my feelings about some of his sexual expectations. Angry, he stormed out of the house.

When he returned hours later, he informed me God revealed to him that he deserved what he asked of me because he waited so long for me.

To pressure me sexually, my husband used many psychological games, including guilt. Playing on my sympathy, he indicated he was deeply spiritual and his ministerial pressures were immense, that his needs were greater than the average man's. After sacrificing so much and waiting so long, he "deserved me" because, in his words, he "could have had a harem." I was an object, a neat little package tied up with a bow, a token of God's appreciation for my husband's sacrifice and hardships. With the immense pressure, refusing his requests was impossible.

Ironically, my husband also used Scripture to sexually pressure or manipulate me. After all, the Bible says our bodies are not our own but belong to our spouse (1 Corinthians 7:4) and that the marriage bed is undefiled (Hebrews 13:4). With those Scriptures in mind, I was convinced my body was his to do with as he pleased.

Porn Queen

A few years into our marriage, I learned my husband was addicted to pornography—a common problem for many abusers according to abused women with whom I have worked. I realized my husband's mysterious disappearances were evidence of his need to get away to feed his sex addiction, including porn and strip clubs. Eventually, his indulgences included me.

During the first few months of our marriage, my husband became fascinated with photo sessions in our bedroom. He was the photographer; I was the subject. Complete with wardrobe changes and explicit positions, these marathon sessions were purely for his enjoyment—they were nothing about love being expressed sexually. These photo times fed his insatiable appetite for pornography. With the introduction of the VHS home video camera, our photography encounters evolved into entire film sessions—lasting from morning to late at night. My husband spent hours writing scripts and purchasing construction floodlights and tripods for our films. As though he were being paid millions of dollars for his productions, he became lost in his fantasy world; he would adjust the lighting with every scene and check the camera angle and focus to ensure he captured every lurid detail. Coached to speak and act in ways completely contrary to my character, I was humiliated.

I WAS HUMILIATED. I WAS REMORSEFUL. THE OBJECT OF HIS OBSESSION, I BECAME HIS PORN QUEEN.

I was remorseful. The object of his obsession, I became his porn queen.

He needed "special" items for his sexual fantasy films, but he couldn't risk being seen in a novelty shop. Instead, I became his gopher, sent to purchase the disgusting "toys" on his detailed shopping list and using only cash to avoid a paper trail. Increasing my humiliation, he made me wear a disguise to places the likes of which I'd never seen. Feeling sleazy, filthy, disgusted, as though traversing Satan's den, I followed his instructions to the letter.

The camera became a regular fixture in our lives. Even in planning getaways together, he insisted on packing it. Once when I objected he threw a tantrum, prompting me to take it along to appease him. He always got his way. His fascination with filming sex and indulging in porn pressured me even more to conform to his wishes, as though inviting a third party into our sex life and taking me deeper into his lurid world.

Escalated Pornography

As his sexual obsession increased, he was always pursuing new fantasies. In the process he chipped away at my resistance by coercing, condoning, and intimidating. When our photo and video sessions ceased to satisfy, he insisted I watch porn with him, at first viewing women undressing. Trying to ease my conscience, he said he was only fantasizing about and viewing the beauty of how God made women sexually—yes, he even used God as leverage against my resistance. Faced with his threats and intimidation, I unwillingly relented so as to avoid his rage, the basis for most of my decisions. Pornography invaded many facets of our lives. Sometimes when he and I traveled, he purchased televisions with built-in DVD players, only to return them for a refund after his appetite was satisfied. Typical of porn addiction, the initial level of pornography eventually wasn't enough to satisfy my husband's desires, and eventually we began watching the most degrading sex acts imaginable. Although never stooping to child pornography, he did like watching high school and college-age girls being exploited. He especially liked the "girl on girl" scenes, and he would instruct me to talk about their young age. With my heart heavily convicted and my stomach wrenching in disgust, at times I would beg him to turn off the porn—all the while knowing that when he eventually turned it on again, the next film would be even more disgusting than the one before. Every time I thought he moved past this obsession, it reared its ugly head again. Nevertheless, I clung to the irrational belief that he would eventually be fulfilled.

As his sexual appetite increased, so did the excuses for his pornographic indulgences. I remember sitting in a library parking lot one day as he began manipulating Scripture to condone his use of pornography. On this occasion, he used the Hebrews 13:4 verse about the "marriage bed being undefiled," deliberately but vaguely misusing it to suggest porn in the marriage bedroom is somehow sanctioned. I seem to recall his suggesting his pornographic habits were better than having an affair. Such conversations were so jumbled, leaving me often thinking, in bewilderment, "What did he just say?" Despite my objections, he made me think I was wrong. Sadly, I caved. Though gradually tapering off in our marriage's final years, this sexual manipulation lasted for years and did untold damage to my psyche, self-worth, and spiritual welfare.

As in all other areas of my life, my codependent behavior permeated our sex life. Like appeasing a screaming child throwing a tantrum, I tried to avoid his anger by dangling sex and pornography before him. Many times my ploys worked, and his anger was held at bay.

However, one particular episode unleashed an inexplicable nightmare. Sitting in a restaurant in a small town in Texas, I could feel turmoil bubbling and boiling like a cauldron in the pit of my stomach, which I always felt before an explosive incident. Sadly, I resorted to offering him porn. He suddenly burst into a rage, demonically growling through his gritted teeth, "What do you want from me?!" With the restaurant full of people, there was no hiding his exhibition. My humiliation increased as he jumped up from the table and grabbed the shirt he was wearing, slowly and dramatically ripping it down the front from the collar to the waist. He stormed out of the restaurant wearing only a partial shirt left hanging around his shoulders. Feeling every eye in the place glaring in concern, I sheepishly followed him to the car.

Surprisingly, no one in the restaurant said a word, not even to show concern for my welfare.

Terrified of what was next, I reluctantly climbed into the driver's seat of the car as he demanded I drive. Panicked, I pleaded, "Where do you want me to go?" As I left the parking lot, he screamed that I had better go in the direction he wanted or there would be consequences. As I entered the interstate, he shrieked that I wasn't going in the right direction and finally commanded me to exit and drive into a hotel parking lot.

Still reeling from the shock of what had happened, I helped carry our belongings into the hotel room, including a book entitled *The Dream Giver*, which is about living out the dreams God has placed in our hearts. Because I spent many days reading quotes from the book to my husband in hopes of encouraging him, it was quite meaningful to me. Suddenly grabbing the book and violently ripping it to shreds in my face, he began roaring about the foolishness of dreams—almost challenging me to look at how *my* dreams failed *me*. As I stood there dumbfounded, he climbed into bed without saying a word or even turning on a light.

Sitting alone in the darkness, I realized I was trapped with no relief from his rage and nothing to appease him. Suddenly, I felt cheated. I had compromised my values and was left shattered—ripped into pieces like the pages of my precious book—clueless as to how I could be put back together. Unfortunately, I remained in this cesspool of compromise until it nearly destroyed me.

> SITTING ALONE IN THE DARKNESS, I REALIZED I WAS TRAPPED WITH NO RELIEF FROM HIS RAGE AND NOTHING TO APPEASE HIM. SUDDENLY, I FELT CHEATED.

Strip Club

Over the years the onscreen sexual performances eventually became inadequate to fulfill his appetite, and he became craftier in his indulgences. After his usual ritual of baiting and grooming me with lavish gifts or taking me to nice places to "spoil" me, he would then ask for another sexual favor. One evening he treated me to a concert, a gourmet dinner, and a fancy hotel room in a big city not far from where we lived. (For fear of being found out, we never indulged in his sexual schemes in the city where we lived.) I should have recognized his ulterior motive for these romantic gestures. When he told me of his plans the next morning, I felt I'd been kicked in the stomach and vehemently objected. However, true to form, he coerced me into shopping for an outfit for a disguise, part of his plan of taking me to a strip club later in the evening. We went incognito to avoid being recognized. Caught completely off guard, I knew I would be guilt-ridden if I refused because of what he had done for me the night before.

Very much at ease when we walked into the club, he'd obviously been there before. On the other hand, I was miserable and a nervous wreck. Sickened by "the show," my compassion overflowed for the women being objectified; they were on display, like cattle at an auction, performing sleazy acts for dollar bills. On the other hand, I was disgusted at the men making their requests as they handed the women the money. Almost immediately after the show started I burst into tears, furious at being coaxed to such a place, furious at these men and their sick minds, and furious at the circumstances leading these women to publicly demean themselves.

"I'm leaving!" I screamed. Shocked at my courage, I ran out of the building, not caring about any commotion I had caused or if I made my husband angry. Bewildered, he followed me to the car. Surprisingly, he wasn't angry; he did express his disappointment as we drove away. As I tried to process what had just occurred, we rode home in silence.

Preacher Pedophile

Always pursuing a new sexual fantasy, one day my husband asked me to go shopping with him. He revealed he'd been going to stores and asking teenage salesgirls to help him choose outfits for me, including asking them to try them on. However, these shopping trips were not about buying me an outfit but about fulfilling his fantasy of girls modeling for him. To add to the "fun," I was to join him while he watched girls select clothes for me. Pressured into obeying him, I went once—that was all that was needed to make me feel foolish and exploited.

Before I knew about his shopping scheme, he bought me a nice bracelet from a beautiful salesclerk at a jewelry store after asking her to try on ankle bracelets and other jewelry. He even audaciously invited her to our home for a Bible study, and she and I became friends. Unaware of how they met until months later, I regretted the way she'd been used.

I didn't realize how far he'd pushed the limits with his shopping sprees until after I left the marriage. Unknown to me, he had been playing his little games at a popular outdoor shopping mall in Louisiana where he was having high school girls try on clothes for him with the explanation that he would send me in to purchase them. They became suspicious when I never came in. Once, after he touched a teenage girl's feet inappropriately in another store in the same mall when she tried on shoes for him, a shopping mall's security guards were alerted to escort him off the property if he was ever seen there again. My husband's ridiculous schemes to satisfy his sexual urges became notorious with outsiders long before I left. In fact, he became known at the mall as "the preacher pedophile." I cannot imagine the shame my son John must have felt when he questioned the salesgirl and confirmed his father's inappropriate behavior. (John later told me that story.) I was not aware of this fiasco until after I left the marriage.

My husband's tendencies to act inappropriately with underage girls were more evident and widespread than I realized. Interestingly, a young woman—the daughter of family friends—informed me of a situation that occurred in the latter years of our marriage, when she just 13. My husband took a "special liking" to her, calling her his "little Michele," commented about her beauty, and marked passages in her Bible about marriage and sexual purity. One day while they were outside alone, he swooped her in his arms, sat her on the hood of the car, and began kissing her cheeks profusely, all the while commenting how his "little Michele" was becoming a woman. When her father stepped out of the house, my husband abruptly whisked her off the car and set her on the ground. Though the experience troubled her, she simply disregarded it as "odd" in trying to come to terms with it.

As I look back through the years, I should have seen the signs and been more sensitive when incidents like these raised red flags in my mind. However, I had been groomed from the time I was actually one of his underage conquests; therefore these scenarios were all completely normal in my mind. I often think to myself: How could I have been so deceived?

The Shame of It All

I've shared my story about the sexual exploitation and abuse in my marriage to illustrate how such deviance exists—even in Christian marriages. These stories only touch the hem of the garment of what I endured. Certain memories of the twisted nature of some of my experiences I just can't share because they are too revolting. Ironically, sexual sin was one area my husband adamantly condemned in his preaching. A friend of mine once said, "Michele, I can identify your husband's weaknesses based on his sermon topics: lust, pride, and anger." She was right, and those weaknesses infiltrated every realm of our marriage.

The sexual abuse played havoc with my mind resulting in guilt, shame, and depression that affected every part of my life. I also suffered from paranoia resulting from compromising my values. I began dreaming I was being watched while I slept—all because my behavior warred against my core beliefs. Next came lethargy and then acceptance, and these things at least eased some of the misery but resulted in my losing the will to fight and neglecting my spiritual and emotional well-being. Acceptance also opened the gate for the enemy to claim more territory in my heart and soul. Turning me into an obedient robot, the abuse poisoned my every fiber, destroyed my self-worth, and left me an empty shell. "Your wish is my command" became, for me, not just a saying but a survival tactic.

Toward the end of our marriage, my husband's requests for me to participate in pornography dissipated, perhaps because of the guilt he felt, though he still engaged in it. Relieved I was no longer forced to participate in his addiction, I didn't care that he was still involved. Despair and hopelessness gradually destroyed any concern I felt for his behavior or life in general as, day by day, I became emptier and grew more disillusioned.

A final note in this chapter. Anyone hearing my story may undoubtedly be left thinking: How could she have stooped to porn? I would never do such a thing! I have no answer for this

THIS IS MY STORY OF ASHES TRANSFORMED INTO BEAUTY. THROUGH THE REDEEMING POWER OF JESUS, I HAVE RECLAIMED WHAT I LOST.

except that I regret many choices I made during those dark years, and I know they were made from sheer survival instinct. Learning the hard way how compromising perpetuates darkness, I am determined to never again compromise my values. This is my story of ashes transformed into beauty. Through the redeeming power of Jesus, I have reclaimed what I lost. Victory in Jesus!

Spiritual Abuse

"Be of the same mind toward one another; do not be haughty in mind, but associate with the lowly. Do not be wise in your own estimation" (Romans 12:9, 10).

Legalism and Spiritual Abuse

Although my heart's desire has always been to please God, my desire became toxic—poisoned by legalism exacerbated by spiritual abuse. *Legalism* is a religious system of thought characterized by strict adherence to the letter of the law (rather than living according to the Holy Spirit's guidance), thereby gaining salvation by being *good enough;* the more good works, the more the assurance of salvation. Therefore, legalism in the extreme sense also breeds entitlement in a narcissist who thinks, *Because I behave well, I am superior.* Another characteristic of legalism is the attempt to decree the salvation of another person by judging—presumably aligning one's judgment with God's. Used as a weapon of manipulation, legalism can result in spiritual abuse—as was the case of my relationship with my husband. Living in a world of polar extremes brought on by my husband's legalism and spiritual abuse, my "normal" was a tangled maze of questions and constantly changing boundaries and standards he dictated. In turn, my insecurities ran rampant, my anxieties mounted, and my habitual fears became overwhelming.

Heavily influenced by legalism in my misguided concept of a vengeful God and motivated by the mind-set that I must be "good enough" to escape His judgment, I was a prime candidate for my husband to spiritually abuse me. Unfortunately, this abuse began influencing my thinking and caused me to doubt my salvation. My surrender to God translated into surrender to my husband; the need to please both God and my husband consumed me. Desperate to conform to anything my husband said was true, I agonized over what I did wrong; Satan seized the opportunity to torture me constantly with anxiety and doubt.

Although I cultivated a relationship with God, it was not based on trust in Him. Because my perception of God was distorted and heavily influenced by my relationship with my husband, my relationship with God became largely performance-based. When I went out of town my husband interrogated me, quizzing me on whether I spent time in God's Word while I was gone—as if he were my conscience on the subject. Afraid of his examination of my Bible reading, I dutifully read a verse or two each day so I could answer truthfully when asked. If I didn't perform to a certain standard, even in the smallest matters, I believed God would withhold His love for me, and my salvation would be left teetering on an extremely thin tether. My legalistic view of a relationship with God combined with the overbearing, abusive chastisement from my husband for the slightest infringement of his rules. God's laws became a living nightmare.

Feeling I was losing my mind, I was desperate for relief. In an insanely misguided effort to please God, I was baptized four times in just a few weeks as a result of my husband's influence. With only him present at the baptisms, he would ask, as I stood in the water, "Do you feel you are saved now?"

> MY SURRENDER TO GOD TRANSLATED INTO SURRENDER TO MY HUSBAND; THE NEED TO PLEASE BOTH GOD AND MY HUSBAND CONSUMED ME.

Questions flooded my mind: *Do I feel the way I'm supposed to feel? Do I have the correct thoughts? Am I mentally reciting the right verses?*

During this time of spiritual turmoil, my husband set himself up as the standard by which I measured my salvation. He would repeatedly taunt me: "Are you saved, or aren't you?" At one point I experienced debilitating pain and was rushed to the doctor. Although the diagnosis was a kidney stone, my husband suggested the pain was a warning from God because of my failure to reach a decision about my salvation. A few days later, to force me into a resolve, he canceled a trip scheduled to visit my parents and grandparents at Thanksgiving. He became my conscience, my judge, and—in a twisted sense—my savior through whom my salvation would be confirmed or denied.

As the years passed the spiritual abuse expanded to our sons. Knowing severe punishment was imminent if they crossed the line, they lived in constant fear. With lust being my husband's deep-seated vice, he was incessantly overbearing in his attempts to ensure my sons were "protected" from it. As a small child afraid of the consequences of seeing something he shouldn't, John ran to hide behind a chair when a girl in a bathing suit flashed on the TV. My young son's unusually distorted concept of the biblical meaning of lust was propagated because of his father's legalistic extremities.

When my sons were very young, they were regularly pressured with

KNOWING THEY WOULD SUFFER MY HUSBAND'S ANGER FOR NOT DOING SO, MY SONS READ THEIR BIBLE EVERY MORNING— OUT OF FEAR.

the question, "Did you read your Bible today?" Knowing they would suffer my husband's anger for not doing so, my sons read their Bible every morning—out of fear. As my sons grew, he interrogated them: "Did you share Jesus with someone today? Who was it?" Again, they were frightened into doing what should have been taught through loving example. Repeatedly forcing them to learn Bible verses and quote them in front of others, to speak publicly, or to be video recorded, he promoted the boys as credits to the wonderful, spiritual father he was. Pawns used to propagate his narcissist tendencies, my sons became exhausted by the pressure to perform.

Effect on Our Families

Extremely quick to impose legalism, my husband excluded people from his inner circle if they didn't do what he said or if they committed what he perceived to be even the smallest infraction. Using Scripture to pronounce judgment—especially on those who saw through his façade or challenged his control—he ensured his circle became smaller as more relationships became casualties of his judgmental tendencies and spiritual abuse.

My husband's legalism and spiritual abuse extended to my family. He threatened my parents many times, suggesting they would never see me or their grandsons again if they did not adhere to his admonishments and align their actions and beliefs with his. When he began controlling my interaction with my family, it was easier to tolerate if I focused on ways they maligned or disobeyed God—even if my husband had fabricated them. In the later years of our marriage, when John was no longer at home, my husband succeeded in isolating Seth and me from my family. Through situations too lengthy and sordid to detail, my husband attempted to alienate us from my family. For about a year Seth and I were not allowed to see them, nor could we communicate with them without my husband's approval. When we received written communication from them, we were forced to show it to him; he would then either dictate or approve any response. Even gifts my family sent us and acknowledgement of those gifts had to be "approved." He also limited the contact Seth and I could have with John, my daughter-in-law, and my granddaughter. When my mom mailed Seth a batch of homemade cookies, my husband became irate when he learned Seth ate them without his approval. Sounds absurd, I know, but it's true. A tradition my mom began when my children were young, her sentimental gesture of sending cookies was twisted into my husband's pursuit for control. When Seth—a straight-A college student—wrote his grandparents a letter to thank them, my husband sat beside him dictating every word, transforming the message into a confrontation rather than a thank you note. Not understanding how brainwashed we had become, and because he chipped away at our resistance for so many years, we obeyed without question. To a degree we recognized how twisted his behavior was, yet we found ways to agree with him in order to help us cope. Clearly, we were was as sick as my husband at this point.

My husband's family members also were victims of his spiritual abuse. He had an eerie control over his mother and father, and they obeyed him in everything just as I did. When he first came to believe he was God's evangelist to the world, he instilled tremendous fear in his mother when he expressed that God had revealed to him that his father might die if there weren't some spiritual changes in their relationship—his father should take more of the spiritual lead and his mother be more submissive. He demanded she get on her knees and pray for forgiveness to avoid God's judgment on their household. Somehow he believed he had the God-ordained right to demand subjugation from nearly everyone with whom he came in contact.

Two more of his family members, an aunt and uncle, were victims of my husband's legalism when they ignored his insistence that they give up smoking. He eventually withdrew from them, including demanding his aunt break fellowship from the church where he preached—a church she had grown to love. Citing Scripture to support his actions, we didn't see either of them for years. Sadly, my husband's uncle died without the dispute being resolved. When their last conversation turned to his uncle's smoking, my husband heatedly argued his uncle's salvation was in jeopardy. Rather than showing concern for the spiritual welfare of the man, my husband insisted he submit to his wishes. His uncle died with the conversation being their last; my husband never relented.

Effect on My Husband

Even my husband was a victim of self-imposed legalism. This was evidenced one day early in our marriage when he disappeared for several hours. When he finally came home, I sensed something was wrong. Later in the evening when he removed his shirt, I was horrified to see his back was completely covered in welts and bruises spreading from shoulder to shoulder and neck to waist. When I inquired what happened, his answer shocked and sickened me. He explained how a particular sin plagued him so much he sought to do penance. In a shady part of town, he encountered a homeless man sitting in an alley and made a bizarre deal: he paid the man twenty dollars to beat him as hard as he could with a belt! My mind swirled in utter disbelief as I imagined the scenario and thought: What kind of tortured mind makes such a request? How could someone devise such a plan?

Reminded of this incident every time I looked at his back, I felt it was done at least partially for my benefit. In light of his coercive attempts in the past, my perception of his reasoning for the incident was an exploitation of my sympathy. If he would go to such lengths to prove his remorse, how could I ever question his sincerity? A torrent of emotion overwhelmed my heart—sympathy, anger, sadness, fear. Feeling trapped and alone, I thought I could never tell anyone. More importantly, I wondered how far would he go in other circumstances. Instead of an act of sincere repentance, his actions were what seemed to be a self-absorbed attempt to ease his conscience and prove his sorrow—a "shock factor" designed to impress and manipulate me and, to a degree, God. Lastly even, himself.

Church Abuse

"Shepherd the flock of God among you, exercising oversight not under compulsion, but voluntarily, according to the will of God; and not for sordid gain, but with eagerness; nor yet as lording it over those allotted to your charge, but proving to be examples to the flock" (1 Peter 5:2, 3).

Schemes Revealed

Being enchanted by the charms of a narcissistic minister—especially a gifted public speaker—a church, unfortunately, can also become a collective victim of abuse. My husband used his gifts and charisma to his advantage. In fact, some of his characteristics have been compared to those of Jim Jones, the infamous religious cult leader of the 1970s. At times he tried to gain control by coercing members to side with him against the church leadership. When a church recognized his unacceptable behavior or began diminishing his authority, he would leave or threaten to leave. This scenario played out in nearly all fifteen churches where we ministered. In fact, my husband left only two of those churches without some sort of negative incident or self-serving motive.

MOVING MORE THAN TWENTY-FIVE TIMES DURING OUR THIRTY-YEAR MARRIAGE, WE REMAINED AT CHURCHES FOR RELATIVELY SHORT PERIODS, USUALLY NO MORE THAN ONE TO THREE YEARS.

Moving more than twenty-five times during our thirty-year marriage, we remained at churches for relatively short periods, usually no more than one to three years. Most of those moves were church related: my husband would become bored; he would be asked to keep office hours and account for his time; he didn't feel free to travel; he devised a new scheme he wanted to pursue; a church member questioned his authority.

With each of our moves to another church, his abuse of church leaders escalated. In fact, at a church in Louisiana, he attempted to publicly defame a dearly loved elder, and this resulted in my husband losing face. Seeing through my husband's self-righteous façade, this elder identified his weaknesses with pornography and narcissism—something no one else in church leadership ever attempted. A ridiculous scheme of my husband's backfired, sending him scurrying in humiliation. Although I should have recognized something was very wrong with him, I often thought the churches were at fault. This indicated how irrational my thinking had become and how sick an abuse victim can be.

Determined to have his way, my husband wanted as little responsibility as possible while still receiving a paycheck. He wanted to be an evangelist and travel the country preaching the gospel to avoid having to answer for his daily activities. When one church didn't comply with his vision, he traveled to see a doctor in another state, a friend, and convinced him to write a letter stating a past illness left him with chronic fatigue syndrome. According to the letter, the only job my husband could perform was traveling for the ministry, a position in which he'd be unencumbered by regular church duties while still receiving the church's financial support. Still, my husband wasn't satisfied with the letter's wording, and because I was his typist, he insisted I change it to his satisfaction. One of the church elders, a lawyer, suspected the letter was altered and confronted my husband. Having been exposed, my husband could not stay where his integrity would be questioned. Consequently, he left the church immediately. A church that, incidentally, had paid almost $60,000 of debt we had accrued through my husband's irresponsible behavior patterns. When he decided to leave that church, my husband once again had no means to support his family.

The Part I Played

Because I never dared warn churches about my husband's behavior, they would almost always find out, unfortunately, the hard way. Just after I left the marriage, the leaders of the church where my husband was ministering made a decision without his approval and announced it in a Sunday service. Determined to be in control, my husband abruptly announced that Sunday would be his last one preaching there despite how his choice affected people who loved and supported him. After they did everything possible to help him in the weeks following my departure, they were repaid with betrayal. Someone told me after the truth came to light that the church members felt they had been duped. I am heartbroken to have been part of the deception, whether unwillingly or willingly.

Praying my ex-husband will make a positive transformation, I trust God will reveal it to me if it happens. Meanwhile, part of the reason I have written this book is to make amends so more churches won't be duped by similar ministers and patterns, and to expose church abuse for the evil it is.

Finding Freedom

"So if the Son sets you free, you will be free indeed" (John 8:36).

Breaking Free

Breaking free from a toxic marriage is difficult and comes at a price. A shattering and horrific experience, divorce is not part of God's perfect plan. But every victim has the right—the responsibility, even—to be free from a destructive marriage. To save her sanity, her children's emotional well-being, and perhaps even her life or her children's, divorce may be the choice she must make.

Despite doing everything I knew to stay in the marriage, I was finally forced to make that choice.

When I recall the moment I realized the necessity of leaving, so many memories come flooding back—the feelings of despair, the overwhelming thoughts of inferiority, how Satan's destructive lies had influenced my thinking all those years. Questions raced through my mind: What are people going to think? . . . What repercussions am I going to suffer for this decision? . . . How am I going to provide for my needs? . . . How could God ever use me—a broken vessel—for His purposes?

The depth of agony and confusion was unfathomable. With the darkness consuming me, even breathing seemed to demand de-

FEELING USED UP, SPIT OUT, GOOD FOR NOTHING, AND WORTHLESS, I WAS BROKEN. ON THE VERGE OF MENTAL AND EMOTIONAL COLLAPSE, I NEEDED REST AND PEACE.

liberate focus. Feeling used up, spit out, good for nothing, and worthless, I was broken. On the verge of mental and emotional collapse, I needed rest and peace.

Thirty years is a long time to be in a marriage filled with cruelty and insanity. My will to continue living, or the ability to even care, was gone. Exhibiting physical signs of tremendous stress, I was pushed beyond what many could have endured. After the horrific night when my husband chased me in his vehicle, I began experiencing numbness in my arms and hands, panic attacks, and heart issues. I was at the breaking point.

When I finally mustered the courage to confront my husband a few weeks after the wreck, Seth and I met him at a Taco Bell. I informed him I couldn't continue living this way. Since John was across the country, I was grateful Seth was with me; his presence instilled me with courage. Having someone I trusted gave me the support I needed and made all the difference.

As I began unburdening my heart, my husband interjected his reasons, excuses, and stories, and these lasted for hours—accounts of his valiant attempts to be God's servant, sacrificing so much to be the bearer of God's message—as though he were God's answer to human frailty. I suppose he wanted me to say, "I understand. All is forgiven and everything is fine. Let's go home." Having heard his stories so many times, I was weary of hearing them again. He expounded on how he should have protected me in the castle while he was out "fighting the dragon." During his discourse he also reminded me he "could have had a harem"; in other words, he had settled for me. His endless chatter left little time for Seth or me to comment. I just sat there scrunched down in a Taco Bell seat, my head in my hands, watching huge tears plop on the floor at my feet. Anguish was all I could muster.

When the night finally ended, I emphatically declared Seth and I were going to a hotel. He insisted on coming with us, but I refused. As I was getting into the car to leave, my husband leaned in and helped me buckle my seat belt—another seemingly manipulative tactic that made my stomach wretch in disgust. All I could think was how I needed to get away from him.

I can't adequately describe the encounter's effect on me. Just deciding to talk to him was life-altering, but his endless verbal barrage splintered my nerves into a million pieces. When I finally got to the hotel, I collapsed in bed and curled into a fetal position. My entire universe was shifting cataclysmically. Hell's demons were shrieking with delight while Heaven's angels were thundering their war cry. In the midst of this fray, I was utterly disoriented—hostage to my past, terrified of my present, uncertain about my future. My tortured mind reeling, I felt I was going crazy, standing at the edge of a great chasm, screaming for help.

> I WAS UTTERLY DISORIENTED— HOSTAGE TO MY PAST, TERRIFIED OF MY PRESENT, UNCERTAIN ABOUT MY FUTURE.

As I lay crumpled and shattered, the strong and comforting arms of my son wrapped around me. "It's going to be OK, Mama," he gently whispered. My 20-year-old, in my eyes still a boy, had become a man. We had exchanged roles. He was now the comforter and superhero and I the wounded, broken little girl needing restoration and repair. Figuratively speaking, he never left my side over the next several months as I sought to regain some sanity. Only God knows the strength I drew from both of my sons during my painful transition.

I don't remember the rest of that night. However, I know somewhere deep inside I found the strength to carry on.

Knowing my husband wouldn't want a scene in front of my in-laws, who were staying with us for a time, and because he realized Seth supported my decision, I knew at least this small advantage was mine. When I called the next day insisting he and his parents leave the house so I could get my belongings, he agreed without question while not disclosing any information to them. After filling the back of a Suburban with my belongings, and after meeting my husband and in-laws in a Starbucks parking lot to tell them goodbye, Seth and I began the long journey to my parents' home in Texas. Out of college for the summer, he put his plans aside, refusing to let me make the trip alone.

DESPITE ALL MY TEARS, STRUGGLES, AND WEAKNESSES, ONE STEP SHAPED A NEW COURSE FOR MY FUTURE.

Needing to think and rest, I left. I didn't know for how long or if I would return, and I had no idea what the next days or weeks or months would hold. Although the process was only beginning the day we left for Texas, putting the car in drive was the first step. Despite all my tears, struggles, and weaknesses, one step shaped a new course for my future. My parents were angels to be there for me in my pain, and in their home I found the beginning of healing and peace.

Emotional Detoxing

When I left my marriage, I felt lost and alone. I wondered how I could make anything of a life half over and scarred with abuse. Satan kept whispering, "You're tainted, you're useless, you're unworthy, you're less than. You wear a scarlet letter. Look at your past. God can never use you." Utterly terrified and seeking peace, clarity, and healing, I went into hiding— not just from my husband, but from life in general.

When I first sought refuge at my parents' home in Texas, I was actually very sick. While unaware of how sick I was, I began emerging out of the darkness—as if waking from a coma. Realizing for the first time the depth of the madness I had endured, I began sharing details of the abuse with my family. Traumatic and revolting, some of the incidents are too hideous for me to reveal even now. As I opened up, others around me shared what they witnessed, revealing to me I wasn't quite as good at hiding the truth as I thought. This also helped me realize the enabler I had become.

Because I was experiencing Stockholm Syndrome's post-traumatic characteristics, my journey of breaking free mentally and emotionally was as difficult as breaking free physically. "Detoxing" symptoms such as nightmares, insomnia, and flashbacks were regular occurrences; sometimes they caused me to unexpectedly burst into tears. I startled easily, jumping and shouting in fear at the slightest surprise. A phone text from my husband would cause extreme diarrhea, nausea, and flu-like symptoms—sending me to bed for hours at a time.

Awaking many nights screaming from nightmares, I slept with the light on; I felt as though I was smothering in the ominous darkness. Frightening and horrifically sad, the nightmares plagued me for quite a few years after I left.

Somewhere deep inside, I guess, a few fissures still needed mending. Fortunately, as Jesus—the Great Physician, the Mighty Counselor—continued to heal me and give me insight, the manifestations of the abuse became less frequent, enabling me to gain self-awareness and, in turn, help others.

Every victim's journey to healing is different. The healing process, which is part of finding freedom, is not without pain and hard work. Most victims will likely experience an array of post-traumatic stress symptoms. However, recovery is possible with time and proper care, and a bright future can be realized. To every victim I say, "One way or another, you will be OK. Take heart in trusting that hope awaits you."

Miraculous Provision

Leaving my marriage with no job experience, no resume, no apparent job skills, and no idea how to provide for myself, I ventured into navigating the corporate world—a daunting first experience for a bewildered 47-year-old woman. On some days I got dressed up and visited potential employers. With no resume and no job experience to offer, I would understandably never hear back. My sweet parents offered me a place to live and an assurance they would take care of me, but I knew being on my own would be more beneficial for me. Still discovering who I was and what my capabilities were, I knew I must make my own way with God as my only source of provision. Remarkably, His plan was greater than I could imagine.

Years earlier I met a precious girl named Macey, a leasing agent for a luxury apartment community next door to one of the churches where my husband was a minister. Meeting through the unlikely circumstance of returning an elderly gentleman to his apartment building after he wandered to the church building, Macey and I bonded instantly. We remained in contact in subsequent years, but little did I know how God would use our friendship to quite literally save my life when I needed to find a way to be self-sufficient. In the years since our first meeting, Macey became the vice president of a property management company, Nickel Plate Properties. Despite my inexperience, she hired me. She also provided me a luxury apartment, a stable income, and eventually the opportunity to find the man of my dreams, whom I met while working at one of her properties! Transformed into a career, my experience at Nickel Plate will always afford me opportunity for employment in the apartment industry. Macey saved my life in so many ways, and I will always be indebted to her.

The world as I knew it was drastically changing, and with every change I made I became more empowered. For my first real job, I headed to Nashville—Music City USA—where I didn't know a soul, and I began experiencing life on my own. Finally embracing the ability to make my own decisions, I went to bed when I pleased, bought what I wanted at the grocery store, and watched what I wanted on TV—small yet liberating victories. I even highlighted my hair, something I was never allowed to do before. I went everywhere by myself, including to church. Most importantly, I listened to God. For the first time in my adult life, the words were not being filtered through my husband's voice. Additionally, Jesus became my best friend and the true love of my life. A deeper connection with Him afforded me a relationship like I'd never known. I decided no one was ever again going to dictate to me what to think or believe about God or His Word. The Holy Spirit was perfectly capable of giving me insight. During my time of healing and enlightenment I grew as a person more than ever before. Embracing this newfound freedom and learning more about myself every day, I was being transformed.

EMBRACING THIS NEWFOUND FREEDOM AND LEARNING MORE ABOUT MYSELF EVERY DAY, I WAS BEING TRANSFORMED.

There were still plenty of challenges from my past. In a desperate attempt to get me back, my husband played every card he could to manipulate me. Believing reconciliation was going to be on his terms, he made a quick and halfhearted effort at getting counseling. After only two sessions, the non-licensed "counselor" encouraged me to take my husband back, claiming he'd never seen anyone so repentant. I remember thinking: You don't have a clue. When this "counseling" didn't work, my husband decided to make the rounds to family members in a haphazard pursuit of making amends. He was sorry for incidents, he said, but his apologies didn't seem to change who he was or prompt him to acknowledge the gravity of his actions. After visiting family members in various states, he called to say he would swing through and pick me up to bring me home, as if he were referring to ending a vacation. Saying my boss would understand, he expected me to give notice at my job although I had just moved into an apartment and had been at this job for only a week. His expectation clearly indicated to me he hadn't changed, and he didn't have the foggiest notion of the severity of his actions.

His reconciliation schemes failed, and I never spoke to him again. I moved on with my life, confident in my ability to make it on my own.

Growing professionally, I was promoted to corporate marketing manager. Within one year I went from having no skills and nothing to offer to working at a corporate level for a successful company. Most of my associations to that time had been with people within churches. God used this new experience to teach me how to function in the "real world." I learned how to interact with people who looked at the world differently than I did.

During this time I also met my husband, Jeff. A tall, handsome, and shy country boy—unassuming, quiet—he intrigued me. From a distance I observed his work ethic, his stability, and his kind nature. Everything my first husband wasn't, Jeff was content and had nothing to prove. I fell hard. Being an extrovert, I asked him if he wanted to go get something to eat. He simply said "OK," and off we went to Applebee's. The conversation at dinner was simple, so different from what I experienced in my marriage. My ex-husband was seemingly incapable of having a meaningful and "normal" conversation with me—instead he would spew Scripture, be absurdly corny, or ask meaningless questions. Having no clue who I was, what I thought, or what my dreams were, he believed life revolved around him. In contrast, I knew I was sharing time with someone very special that night at Applebee's. Not only falling head over heels in love with Jeff, I really, really *liked* him—and knew almost instantly I wanted to marry him.

Our wedding was in November 2013 in a small log cabin wedding chapel in Gatlinburg, Tennessee, with only the officiant, Jeff, and me present. He has been my rock, my best friend, and the strong arms I run to when I'm tired or sad or just need a hug. Everything I dreamed he would be, Jeff has been integral to my healing, showing me how a man is supposed to treat and love a woman. Sometimes all I have to do is sit next to him and all the world is right. He lets me know everything is going to be OK. I love him with all my heart.

Located in the hills of East Tennessee, our home is small and simple and needs lots of restoration. But it is also full of love and peace and security. So, to me, it is a mansion. God knows the happiness I have known there.

My heart is so full, and I wait with expectation to see what God has in store next.

Healing Through Hope

After some time passed since leaving my nightmarish existence, it occurred to me I couldn't be the only one who has experienced abuse in Christian marriage. Researching the evil and hidden cancer of domestic abuse within the church, I began blogging about what I experienced. The response has been incredible. Women have contacted me from across the world. They have begged me to keep writing because, in telling my story, I have been telling theirs. They have called me courageous and brave, characteristics I never would have attributed to myself. Determined not to let my story or those of other women be wasted, I couldn't let this evil continue without trying to do something—even if only a little something.

Amazingly, my "little something" continues growing, and doors are opening for key connections and opportunities to speak. Hearing my story, women are embracing hope. In the process, God has led me to establish a ministry. Sometimes I am overwhelmed, sometimes just downright scared. Staring Satan in the face, I refuse to back down because he has no authority as long as I don't relinquish it to him. Empowered by God, I pursue this challenging call, trusting the One who dispels my fears and emboldens me. By God's grace I will continue on with dignity, every step being led by Him. Creating purpose out of pain and beauty from ashes, He has gifted me wholeness and healing which has, at times, flickered like a glimmer of hope in the darkness. This is why my blog has this simple name: Hope Glimmering.

> HEARING MY STORY, WOMEN ARE EMBRACING HOPE. IN THE PROCESS, GOD HAS LED ME TO ESTABLISH A MINISTRY.

The Faces of Victimization

"Reflect on what I am saying, for the Lord will give you insight into all this" (2 Timothy 2:7).

What Victims Endure

Tearing at the heart of marriage's sanctity, abuse is no respecter of social status, race, religion, sex, or appearance. Here is another critical truth: abusers are generally people who others least suspect to be capable of abuse. Abused by pastors or church leaders and other respected Christian men, women in supposedly Christian marriages are trapped in scenarios in which the mind games and victimization go much deeper—as was true in my case. Often using God, the Bible, and the church to back them up, abusers manipulate Scripture, religious doctrines, and church leaders to control their victims. Even more despicable is when the abuser is sitting in church cloaked in a pious demeanor while behaving horrendously behind closed doors.

Because they are attempting to do what they believe is the right thing, victims endure the unthinkable for the sake of saving their marriage—an extremely costly choice in terms of their emotional welfare, mental state, and physical safety. Their abuse experiences include name-calling, vile language, proclamations of hatred, punching, choking, being yanked by their hair, child abuse, sexually deviant behavior, death threats, and much more. Believing they are somehow honoring God by suffering and honoring their marriage commitment, victims stay in the marriage for years or even a lifetime—or, sometimes, even give their life through their decision to stay.

Defining Abuse

Another term for abuse is *battering*, and this is manifested in various forms including attacking a victim's physical, mental, emotional, financial, and spiritual well-being. Abusers use everything in their power to gain complete control: fear, manipulation, intimidation, coercion, Scripture, threats, and physical violence. However, an abuser cannot gain control without the victim's cooperation. And that can be withheld through the empowering of recognizing abuse for what it is.

Awareness of the characteristics of abuse certainly would have equipped me to fight. Therefore, allow me to identify some of those characteristics in terms of the victim. She:

- is afraid to express an opinion or is made to feel her opinions are foolish;

- has no say in decisions;

- is called names like stupid and dumb;

- is told she is worthless or can't do anything right;

- is humiliated by her partner;

- witnesses outbursts of rage—punching walls, breaking objects, screaming, driving erratically—and other behaviors jeopardizing safety or well-being;

- is forced to act against her will—whether in public or private, including being coerced into sexual activity which is against her judgment, such as participating in pornography, threesomes, and sadomasochism;

- is made to feel like a slave or the lesser partner in the relationship;

- fears her partner and must walk on eggshells to keep from prompting rage just to try to keep the peace;

- is assaulted, including being pushed, hit, slapped, grabbed, or any other kind of forceful behavior which could be physically or emotionally harmful;

- constantly apologizes for things she did not do;

- is forced to lie or be deceitful with other people to protect her abuser's image;

- fears for her children's physical, mental, emotional, or spiritual well-being because of her abuser;

- feels controlled by her abuser;

- is isolated or alienated by her abuser from friends or family;

- feels mentally manipulated;

- is regularly threatened;

- feels responsible for every bad situation or crisis;

- is accountable to her abuser for her whereabouts, activities, and relationships with others.

As the victim endures different aspects of abuse, she will also experience a continual cycle of her life as a victim. The abuse cycle unfolds in the following stages:

- Impending doom: Becoming dark, moody, and easily angered, the abuser threatens, criticizes, pouts, and is abrasive. Sensing what is coming, the victim goes to extremes to pacify her abuser.

- Eruption: Rage ensues accompanied by physical, mental, and emotional battering. This phase is characterized by punching walls, breaking objects, driving erratically, screaming, threatening, and more.

- Honeymoon period: The abuser claims he is "sorry"; he cries convincingly while making empty promises to change; he usually provides gifts, flowers, physical affection, and verbal affirmation.

- Calm: Life continues calmly as if all is normal, causing the victim to believe the abuse will not reoccur while, at the same time, waiting for "the other shoe to drop." Living in this daily uncertainty causes a disconnect with the reality of her situation, and this can cause her to think, "He's really a good guy." This is certainly a more comfortable belief for the victim to embrace.

A Victim's Mind

Bewildered by the abuse, those who have not experienced it struggle to grasp how it happens and why victims would choose to stay in an abusive relationship. The following thoughts are common: How could they let abuse happen? . . . Why can't they see abusive behavior is crazy? . . . Why don't they leave? . . . It would never happen to me.

Allow me to explain a victim's thinking.

A woman can become a victim for various reasons. Perhaps a series of events has altered her thinking, her emotions, and her sense of well-being. Perhaps her victimization began in childhood or with her need for acceptance at any cost. Perhaps it resulted from choices made arising from the need for sheer survival. Whatever the reason, the victim falls into a trap. Then, when abuse occurs, she begins to expect and accept it, losing pieces of herself as her identity slips away. Lost and in shock, she drowns in a swirling cesspool of fear, insecurity, and confusion.

WHEN SHE TRIES TO UNDERSTAND HERSELF, SHE ENCOUNTERS A VOID BECAUSE SHE HAS LOST HER IDENTITY.

When she tries to understand herself, she encounters a void because she has lost her identity.

If she decides to break free, she has no idea who she is because victimization has defined her. Consequently, in facing the daunting task of putting her life back together, she doesn't know how to begin.

I cannot overemphasize this fact: *A victim does not see herself as a victim.* After being groomed, deceived, and manipulated by the abuser's charms, gifts, and compliments, she is initially blindsided by the abuse, eventually becoming accustomed to it. Failing to recognize the trauma she is experiencing, she becomes a victim. A friend of mine compares abuse to placing a frog in a pot of cold water and gradually turning up the heat. Because the heating process is so gradual, the frog does not realize it is being boiled alive and makes no effort to escape. In comparison, victims continue in the same cycle day after day until it becomes a way of life. Before they realize how miserable they are, ten, twenty, even thirty years have passed. Bound in chains forged by physical, mental, emotional, verbal, and spiritual forces, the victim is resolved to "stick it out" regardless of the horrible cost she is paying.

As a prisoner of those chains, I didn't see a way out until I realized I might lose my life if I stayed. Even then I didn't perceive myself as an abuse victim; this is a lack of awareness

I have found with most abuse victims. I felt the pain and suffered the trauma, but I didn't realize it was named "abuse" because my abuser never hit me.

Let me provide a glimpse into an abuse victim's daily existence. A conversation with her partner becomes bizarre, then manipulative and controlling, then explosive. The victim reels in confusion, utter torment, and most of all fear. Conflicted regarding how to respond and knowing she will ultimately be blamed, she thinks of ways to defuse the situation. Next, believing the problem is her fault, she is guilt-ridden. Spending the next hours or days or months groveling for forgiveness, she hopes for some shred of approval indicating she finally stands in good graces. As moments of relief break through, she is overwhelmed with euphoria and gratefulness, basking in those emotions—until the horror returns. Temporarily relieved, she can't afford to spend time wondering what will trigger the next episode. Ironically, this cycle is the only constant in the victim's life.

As time slips away and the victim plunges deeper into victimization, she rationalizes her situation. Her conversation with herself goes something like this: "It's my fault. He's just having a bad day. What about yesterday when he brought me flowers? I'm the one who's crazy. I'm the failure. This isn't really him. I need to fix this. I can't let this marriage fail. I am too far in to leave now. If I'm doing what Jesus says, I will have mercy and suffer for doing what's right. Marriage is forever. God wants me to stay." The rationalizations are unending.

In my case, I would have thoughts like this: "He quotes God's Word. So many people tell me how wonderful he is and how lucky I am. He's a minister, a man of God. He's sincere. He's just under pressure." I was overwhelmed with guilt, shame, and fear; I believed I was the failure. And when I finally faced the reality that I must get out, my mind reeled with questions: What will happen to the church? Will I cause people to lose their faith? Will I leave a negative legacy about Christ and His church? Will I go to hell?

While victims are among the most resilient individuals imaginable, they are also fragile. Enduring incredible trauma, they survive—but often at the expense of their mental, emotional, spiritual, and physical well-being. Void of life, will, and spirit, they feel hopeless; their strength slips away. Numb, empty, and afraid, they fall into despair, and this affects their choices.

As abuse slowly chips away at their identity and sense of self-worth, victims will turn to almost any false comfort just to "feel something." Many victims turn to alcohol or drugs or immoral relationships for merely a moment of comfort or freedom from pain; many sink into deep depression; some become physically sick or disabled, spending most of their time in bed simply trying to survive. Some develop eating/purging disorders. Unfortunately, some have committed suicide to end the madness, and in the most horrific of circumstances, some have resorted to murder in a desperate attempt for relief.

TORMENTED BY AN INDESCRIBABLE DEPRESSION DURING THE LAST TWO YEARS OF MY MARRIAGE, I EVENTUALLY WITHDREW INTO MYSELF, AN EMOTIONALLY DANGEROUS PLACE TO EXIST.

Looking back, I realize I was so adversely affected by my situation that I made choices which allowed me to *feel* in control—at least for the moment. For example, I regularly consumed medicinal citrus electrolyte drinks to purge my system in an effort to lose weight. Tormented by an indescribable depression during the last two years of my marriage, I eventually withdrew into myself, an emotionally dangerous place to exist.

Finally realizing God did not intend for me to live in such a way, I began to trust that He was sheltering me in the palm of His hand. Unfortunately, I lived in fear of what other people thought of me, believing people's thoughts were God's thoughts. But I began to realize that because no one else walked in my shoes, God was the only one to whom I was accountable, and that thought began to set me free. Retraining my thinking, I realized I was strong for finally deciding, "No more. *Enough.*" Now living empowered, I want others to know it's OK to leave, that they will survive, and that God will strengthen them in the process.

Other Victims' Stories

Many victims have reached out to me for connection, for someone to listen, for encouragement and advice. In short, they cry out to be understood. Giving voice to their cries, I want to share excerpts from a few of their stories to heighten awareness of the mind-set of the victim as they navigate their confusing world while trying to remain faithful to what they believe to be true. Names and locations have been changed to protect their privacy. Some of the following passages are direct quotes from these brave women. Be advised: this content may include emotional triggers for some readers.

Angie: Angie was married to a minister who verbally, sexually, physically, mentally, and spiritually abused her for more than twenty years. On many occasions he claimed he hated her, that she was fat, and she was not what he wanted. Once when she refused sex with him, he raped her, reading Bible verses out loud while sitting on top of her. When she was pregnant he shoved her into a bathtub, fracturing her arm. He was often verbally abusive with both his wife and children.

Janet: Janet and her husband attended the same church for more than twenty years. When she tried to expose his abusive behavior she was treated as a troublemaker despite having lived above approach for many years. Her abuse included her husband choking her in front of her daughter, giving her a black eye, dragging her around by her hair, running her daughter down with a golf cart, and much more. He brandished a gun to frighten a friend who was trying to help Janet. A loved and respected church member, this abuser endeared himself to other church members through various favors. His abusive behavior was never addressed apart from his receiving a couple of "counseling" sessions and invitations to a marriage enrichment class.

When he decided to file for divorce, he locked Janet out of the house eight times, each time keeping her from retrieving her belongings. A police officer responding to one of those episodes was also abusive, telling Janet she was a nuisance. Throughout the separation and divorce, and even after the divorce, the abuse continued and even escalated. The stories are horrifying, nightmarish. (I won't account them here to avoid legal and privacy issues for the victims involved.) However, I will say there were some covert attempts on Janet's life including suspicions of poisoning. Many times I have been concerned for her and her children's physical safety.

Only receiving about eight hundred dollars from her husband in a year, she struggled to feed herself and her daughter. One time when I spoke with her, she and her daughter were hungry and had to share an order of tater tots from a fast-food establishment just to have something to eat. Still, no one seemed to believe her, no one offered food or financial help, and no one checked on her or her daughter.

Pamela: Pamela's husband was known as the good ol' boy in the church. Everyone loved him.

The following is a directly quoted message I received from Pamela:

> I keep thinking I have to tell you this. My kids have no idea. Their dad, my first husband, was abusive, but only when we were alone. He was a completely different person when the two of us were together with no one else. He was addicted to pornography. I kept finding piles of porn magazines and other things, and there was always an explanation. "It belongs to 'so and so' and he left it in my car . . . " Ad infinitum, ad nauseum. I have never, ever told anyone this before.

> I'm a wreck telling you. No one would have ever believed me, and sometimes things were good, and I managed to stay married for many years. The day he died was very hard for everyone, but I felt this load lifting and leaving me and [I had] no idea it was so heavy because I'd been carrying it so long. My kids can never ever know this.

> One thing which happened to me through those years is I never properly became a mature adult. I never

functioned emotionally or socially as an adult because there was no room to grow. Walking on eggshells and living to please and hoping I didn't make him mad because he was so jealous . . . it's all that drove me.

God help me, I wouldn't have known how to escape even if I tried. I was told if I left, I'd be killed.

Donna: Donna was an artist working for major film companies in Hollywood. She obtained a graduate degree from a prestigious seminary. Her "Christian" husband stole more than two million dollars from her, leaving her penniless with nowhere to go. He also tried to kill her seven different ways, but he was so secretive in the way he did things that she was unaware of some of the attempts until after she left. When she did leave, she was homeless for two years, living in a tent and then a camper. Unable to afford food, she lost 50 pounds from sheer hunger. She found most shelters were reserved for women with children, and there was a wait-list. She fell through the cracks in the system. When she went to her church for help, she was forced to fill out an "application of need" and told it could be six months before she would receive assistance. Although she had been a member of this massive church for twenty years and given thousands of dollars to the offering, she was denied help when she desperately needed it.

Lillian: Lillian's husband installed spyware on all her electronics so he could track her texts, calls, transactions, and Internet searches as well as her every move. He became so abusive she began fearing for her life. One of her most chilling memories is seeing him standing in front of the bathroom mirror with a dark, blank look in his eyes. In an evil voice he growled, "I am Satan."

Melinda: She relates her awful struggle in her words:

I have been looking for the answers to what happened to me. Drank my way into a treatment center. This may be the missing piece of my story leading me to the bottom. Hope you can give me some direction on this taboo subject. He [the abuser] has gone on to do very well. I, however, have struggled. Thank you for pointing me somewhere to learn about my experience and why I have paid such a heavy price in all areas of my life. I was afraid of him leaving me.

Once I was sick with PID (pelvic inflammatory disease) and unavailable sexually, and he told me he did not sign up for this. I cannot tell you the unimaginable things I let him do and how sick I became mentally. I drank and drank and told myself this was normal. Some things actually became addictive behavior intertwined with my addiction to alcohol. Treating me like a sex toy was the norm. I thought it gave me power. It was sadomasochistic behavior . . . thank God I did not die!

Gloria: Although I never met Gloria, her daughter Sherry communicated the horrors of Gloria's thirty-nine years of abuse. Gloria was married nearly four decades to a beloved and respected preacher in perhaps the largest church denomination in the United States during the "tent revival" days. She was beaten regularly. Once, to escape being beaten to death, Gloria grabbed her little son and ran to the tent where her husband was scheduled to preach that night.

Sherry shared with me her memory of being a small child witnessing her father slamming her mother against the wall, holding a knife to her neck, and threatening to slit her throat. After running to a neighbor who called the police, Sherry was severely reprimanded by her father for exposing him. Although he never physically abused her, he once lunged for her; her brother intervened, exclaiming, "If you touch her, I will kill you!"

Sherry's father also engaged in multiple affairs; one lasted sixteen years. When the affair was exposed, his preaching career ended along with his marriage. After Gloria's death, Sherry found some of her mother's journals, one of which she shared with me, a calendar from June 1972. Entries throughout the month included "Jack's birthday," "Tent Revival," "Vacation Bible School," and "Roast at Church." The following is a chilling entry dated June 11, 1972: "James beat me about 11 p.m. Me and Jack [her son] went to [the] tent. James also attempted to murder me." I wept as I read those words. To see those notations in a precious woman's handwriting among all the scheduled church potlucks, vacation Bible school, and birthdays is heartbreaking. On another page she wrote, "Divorce James June 1995—A blessing I did this. Thank God it's now October 29, 2006." Yes, Gloria, thank God. I admire your strength and thank God you are living in eternal bliss, where I will meet you someday.

Sandra: I struggle with Sandra's story because her abuser is still in the ministry and is being endorsed by high-profile Christian speakers and writers unaware of his abuse history. I hope he has changed. If he has, two of his former victims have no knowledge of that change. Sandra's story, quoted directly here, gives insight into how abusers gain control:

> I met Alex when I was 15 and was drawn to his charm and passion for Jesus. He was vocal and unashamed how he followed Christ and befriended anyone on our school's campus, inviting them to church. When we

started dating, I was excited to be in a relationship with a Christian guy. Coming from a past of promiscuity, I figured dating someone this outspoken in their faith would mean I could avoid sexual sin, be treated with worth and value, and have a relationship of integrity and honor.

But the control and the manipulation set in early through his tactics to lead me away from my closest friends and family. He would never want to hang out in groups with my friends and insisted I leave social gatherings to be alone with him. He began by reminding me of how my friends were falling short of what God calls us to in Scripture and [that] I was most likely to sin when I was around them. He acted like he wanted to protect my spiritual state by keeping me away from temptation, when in reality it was in isolation he could control and coerce me best.

Although he talked often about Jesus, led Bible studies, attended seminary, preached from a young age, and even tried to teach me about theology, he operated out of hurt and wounds. The message was conflicting. While he spoke often of Jesus, he wasn't himself set free by Jesus. He controlled to make sure of his power and authority over me.

During our time alone, he would often have us do one-on-one Bible studies, and through this make sure he established his relational and spiritual authority over me. He used tactics of belittling me from the start to make sure I knew I needed him for my new spiritual journey. After all, who else would lead me closer to Christ if he didn't? Who else would love me? I can't quite explain the ways he used my vulnerable state of knowing little about theology and Scripture, guiding me toward what sermons to listen to which served his purposes, or what books to read. I have an innate desire to please God, but we became so intertwined spiritually, so I was often confused if it was more important to please God or Alex. What he was especially crafty at was leading me toward the belief that, in order to please God, I needed to please Alex. This is exactly the twisted mind-set Alex knew would play to his advantage sexually, spiritually, and emotionally.

With everything I would do for the Lord—whether it be teaching a Bible study, reading the Word of God, serving in an apartment ministry, or sharing the gospel—I never knew if I was doing it truly for Christ or for Alex. The two were so closely intertwined that he became my God. And he liked it that way.

During our relationship I was in a constant state of paranoia while I was away from him, making sure my phone was on me at all times when he wasn't around because he would become irate and accusatory when I didn't answer his call or text immediately. Many times he would show up where I was if I didn't answer—not because he cared and was checking on my safety but [because] he wanted to make sure I knew he was aware of what I was doing at all times.

I vividly remember a time a few years into our relationship when I worked at the fitness center on my Baptist college campus. He hated that the majority of the people I worked with were males—specifically males who took care of their physique. He would often make me pay for hours or even days by withholding affection or verbally beating me down after I worked a shift with a male. We had a work Christmas party on campus one evening, and Alex insisted I not attend because he didn't want me around any guys. I'm not sure how I ended up still going, but he made sure it was as uncomfortable and controlled as possible. He was not even a student at my university but came to campus and sat outside the building the entire time during the party, staring into the room to enforce his presence and remind me I was not to talk to any other men. I often would ignore my coworkers who said "hello" because it was better than having to deal with Alex's anger. I ended up quitting the job because Alex didn't want me working there.

That summer I took a six-week job working at a Christian camp about two hours from where we lived. I felt like it would be a great opportunity for me to grow my faith and serve with youth, but Alex made sure my summer was all about him. We had twenty-four hours off each week. Alex urged me that, if I loved him, I would spend my entire time off making the four-hour round-trip home to see him. One weekend when he came to visit, another male camp counselor said, "Hey, Sandra, just wanted to remind you our team debriefing meeting starts in 10 minutes!" Alex pouted and went into fits of depression and rage all weekend, questioning me about why the guy knew my name. On these same days I would often catch him watching porn, or he would convince me to have sex or give sexual favors to him. These requests were clear indications his intentions were far from a genuine concern for my spiritual growth.

I was recently cleaning out my old Facebook messages and found [more than] five people I was close to and those who were simply acquaintances in my life who warned me to get out of the relationship. This doesn't include those who called me, texted me, met with me in person, or wrote me handwritten letters pleading with me to leave.

What brings me the most grief are the years I missed out on serving and following God freely and wholly. I knew about Jesus and wanted to follow Him, but I couldn't seem to grasp grace for what it truly was—the fact it was free. I thought I needed to earn it, to pay penance for all my past sins. Although God didn't require such penance of me, Alex did. He took advantage of my lack of understanding, and instead of shepherding me into freedom and love, he lorded his leadership over me [by] holding a place of authoritative and graceless godship in my life.

Rebecca: Rebecca's husband was a respected military officer, Bible teacher, and leader in the church. Behind closed doors, however, he was violent, abusive, and highly addicted to pornography. Once during an incident when he became angry, he shoved Rebecca's head into a mirror smashing the glass to pieces. During his rages he would throw objects, and one time he barely missed their baby boy's head with a plate. For more than ten years Rebecca tried to hold the marriage together, but his pornography use and the abuse finally dissolved the marriage.

Christine: Christine's story depicts how a woman in the church can feel trapped by both her devotion to being right with God and an abusive marriage. Her torment is reflected in her own words; they are quite disconnected at times as I relay them here because they were compiled from a series of messaged conversations:

I was a preacher's wife for 31.5 years. I was 17 when we married. Six months later (I just turned 18) he hit me the first time. Knowing I'd go to hell for divorcing in the absence of adultery, I stayed; and no one ever knew the things going on in our home. (He was also a police officer, often preaching for small congregations who didn't have full support; so he stayed in law enforcement.) How do you ever tell anyone he hits you when he wears those hats? He preached on lectureships in several states and wrote for several publications.

I finally found the strength to leave in 2011 and divorced. I lost everything. My children would not come with me. The congregation withdrew fellowship from me. My children have nothing to do with me. They will hang up on me if I call. They return my cards, letters, and gifts marked "Refused. Return to sender."

I tried every day to be perfect and not set him off. The years of physical and emotional abuse finally took their toll, and I gave up. I left. I lost nearly everyone I'd known all those years. I am terrified of judgment because I am absolutely certain of my eternal destiny in hell. I no longer worship with the Lord's people. I no longer pray.

I just wanted out. I endured things like him throwing me out of the house, and I slept in the car; throwing me to the floor (but he convinced the kids he was trying to move me into our room, and I tripped). He's quite charismatic and manipulative. Agreeing with him always yielded better results.

Sometimes he would look at the Craigslist "women looking for men" ads. Then there was a time [when he was on duty] he seized porn tapes and magazines and drugs out of a car. The drugs, of course, went into evidence. There was really no reason for him to take the tape and magazines. He made me watch it while we participated in bedroom activities. He called it my "training video" so I could get better. I was a "prude," and if I didn't initiate bedroom events daily, life was miserable.

How did we misjudge so badly? I graduated salutatorian, so I'm not the village idiot. You are bright and intelligent; it's evident in your writing. How could we have made such bad decisions? Funny . . . he's still in the pulpit, and I'm the bad guy.

Many times I thought it would be better if one of us died. Then I would be free, either way. I frequently have nightmares. They are always the same theme. I'm alone. It's dark. Usually [in] our bedroom. And someone is coming through the door to hurt me.

I don't want to be far from God. The simple fear of hell is what kept me in my earthly hell for 31+ years. I'm afraid of everything. For so, so, so many years I was afraid of making a mistake and setting him off. I was afraid of hell. I was afraid to leave. I am afraid to let go of my moorings. I am in a catch-22. And why is divorce a worse sin than any other? His being unkind to me is an OK sin. His being abusive and not cherishing me is an OK sin. But my divorcing him is a big sin. It occurs to me I should have shot him. I could repent of murder and be free to remarry. But because I chose to leave him alive, I am forever condemned to be unmarried.

Doesn't make sense.

I met with a preacher this past Sunday to tell him I would like to go ahead and identify with a congregation, but I needed to tell him I had been disfellowshipped in another church. They will not let me place membership there. I cannot eat with them at potlucks, etc. The preacher said I could keep coming. I need to be in worship, and I want to be in worship. I don't know what to do. I'm back to not going anywhere.

When I finally left, after trying to kill myself, I ended up in a new hell and lost all my family and faithful brethren who'd worked side by side with me for 30 years. Now I am still convinced I have an eternal abode in hell, so I'm not sure what I gained. I have gotten back to feelings of wanting to end all this, but then I'm right back with a sure ticket to hell. I see no way out.

By gaining some insight into these victims' tortured mindsets, you can hopefully understand more fully the labyrinth of abuse and what it does to the mind, spirit, body, and soul. Many victims have suffered much more than I, and their stories are more compelling, but not everyone wants to speak out the way I am because doing so is very hard.

Nevertheless, abuse must be exposed and expelled. But how can a force of this magnitude be confronted? Writing is my way of confronting this evil. As you continue reading, I pray you will find suggestions to help you confront this issue in your church, your friendships, your home, your family. If we each do our part, we can make a huge difference.

NEVERTHELESS, ABUSE MUST BE EXPOSED AND EXPELLED. BUT HOW CAN A FORCE OF THIS MAGNITUDE BE CONFRONTED?

Navigating the Nightmare of Leaving

If you are a victim, in this section I want to speak directly to you. I can't give you an answer regarding when to leave or even if you should; if someone tells you they can, they are sadly mistaken. Furthermore, God's Word simply doesn't address every scenario. Although the Bible encourages us to live as closely as possible to the written Word, sometimes we fall short of God's perfect standards or find ourselves in less than God's ideal circumstances. However, when we live according to the Holy Spirit, hope is available. God gave His Spirit to followers of Jesus so He could reveal His will in every situation.

A person truly seeking God will know when it's time to leave. He will make it very evident. While enduring the nightmare of decisions regarding my own situation, I begged God to *force* me to go back *if it was what He wanted.* However, several times, just when I decided to return to the abuse, He threw open a door in the opposite direction, taking me further away from returning. With every doorway He guided me through, I felt His pleasure and confirmation and watched Him unfold a plan which continues to astound me.

Because of what the Lord has done in my life, I believe He has called me to be a messenger to let you know it's OK to leave a marriage that could destroy you. Notice I said *destroy*—not *dishearten*, which is vastly different. Through hard work, God's divine power, and reputable counseling, hope exists for an unpleasant marriage. In contrast, a destructive marriage is probably hopeless, and you may be forced to leave. If you are honest with yourself and with God, the Holy Spirit will reveal the difference. If you do leave, you will most assuredly have opposition from Satan, other people, your abuser, even yourself. However, if you truly believe you are supposed to leave your abusive relationship, you will leave at almost any cost. You will leave when the abuse becomes bad enough, and you will become resourceful in the process. No comforts of life will be worth staying, and lack of money will not stop you.

TRUST GOD IMPLICITLY; ONLY HE KNOWS THE FUTURE, AND HE HAS ALREADY INITIATED A REDEMPTIVE SOLUTION BY SENDING JESUS.

Desperate times call for desperate measures. The lowliest job will fill you with gratefulness. Trust God implicitly; only He knows the future, and He has already initiated a redemptive solution by sending Jesus.

With your life seemingly in shambles, rebuilding your life, sanity, and identity will be a monumental task filled with fear. Fortunately, the Bible offers comfort and hope. The story of Nehemiah's rebuilding of Jerusalem's wall (detailed in the book of Nehemiah, Chapters 1 through 6, as outlined below) is extremely applicable and encouraging. Here is the background to Nehemiah's story:

Nebuchadnezzar, king of Babylon, invaded Israel, destroying Jerusalem and capturing the surviving Israelites. Annihilated by Nebuchadnezzar's army, the city wall was a pile of rubble, leaving the relative few who remained in the city of Jerusalem vulnerable to attack.

However, when Cyrus of Persia became king, he released the Israelites to rebuild the city. Under the leadership of Nehemiah, a man of God, Israel began reconstruction while experiencing opposition in the form of death threats, lies, and evil schemes. Despite resistance, the wall was completed as a result of faith, endurance, and persistent prayer.

In the same way, invaded by the destructive force of abuse, you can reconstruct the rubble of your life and your broken heart. As you do, you will be bombarded with threats, manipulation, and deception, much like the Israelites experienced. May you find strength, resolution, and comfort in Nehemiah's faith and responsiveness to God's desire for restoration. May you be encouraged by Nehemiah's faith in action. Here are the steps he took, and you can draw the parallels in your life.

1. Nehemiah prayed.

Prayer is essential to your life, especially when leaving an abusive relationship. When I left my marriage, I was consumed by fear, doubt, guilt, shame, and worry—characteristics of all victims' brokenness. Defeated, I was right where Satan wanted me. But the God I serve heard my pleas and answered my prayers for deliverance. Not only did He deliver me from the brokenness, He ushered me, and is continuing to usher me, into an abundance of life, joy, and peace.

2. Nehemiah asked God to hear his prayer.

God always hears your prayers, but asking Him to hear them is an act of your submission from a humble heart. There were times I couldn't understand, and I begged God to help me, in fact pleaded with Him, to make my path clear, to give me wisdom, to hear me. I would have rather died than disobey Him. As I gained a fuller understanding of who He is—a loving Father and compassionate friend, my comforter, guide, counselor, anchor—I shed my concept of a vengeful God who wished to capitalize on my fear of His throwing me into the flames of hell. As a result, my life and my relationship with Him changed forever.

3. Nehemiah confessed to God his sins as well as those of his family and nation.

Reflect on your choices, confessing to God those choices that brought you to your current state or exacerbated your situation. Though I'm not insinuating the abuse is your fault, nor am I trying to inflict guilt, no one is perfect, and the choices and mistakes you've made—no matter how seemingly insignificant—are yours. Own them. The cleansing process of confession prepares you for God's work in answer to your prayers.

> THE CHOICES AND MISTAKES YOU'VE MADE—NO MATTER HOW SEEMINGLY INSIGNIFICANT—ARE YOURS. OWN THEM.

Coming to the same conclusion, I realized some of my choices were not spiritually or emotionally beneficial. Although reasons existed for those choices, the reasons were not excuses. The fact is, I veered from what I knew to be right. Whether because of fear, manipulation, coercion, or just my own weakness, I made bad choices and needed to take responsibility for them. Opening the door for demonic influence in my life by aligning myself with my husband's sins, I allowed Satan to create strongholds, and those needed to be broken. This realization came gradually as I saw the connection between some of my choices and their consequences.

Next, after making amends for your choices, think about your immediate family or family line. Confessing your family's sins releases you from any generational strongholds or soul ties with evil acts or destructive patterns your family members have committed or created. You will be surprised how confession releases you from so much darkness.

When I became aware of confession's power, I began taking stock of decades of generational sins existing in my family line: alcoholism and drug addiction, sexual immorality and infidelity, domestic abuse, and more. I decided to break those strongholds, declaring the patterns would end through confession and deliverance in the name of Jesus and through the cleansing power of His blood shed on the cross. As the Bible clearly states, "For though we live in the world, we do not wage war as the world does. The weapons we fight with are not the weapons of the world. On the contrary, they have divine power to demolish strongholds. We demolish arguments and every pretension that sets itself up against the knowledge of God, and we take captive every thought to make it obedient to Christ" (2 Corinthians 10:3-5). When I embraced the power of breaking strongholds, my life changed. There is so much power available.

Finally, notice Nehemiah took responsibility for confessing the sins of his nation's people. Living in the world taints us—directly and indirectly. Because we live in a fallen world

> YOU WILL BE SURPRISED HOW CONFESSION RELEASES YOU FROM SO MUCH DARKNESS.

in which Satan seeks to wreak havoc, we must deal with the consequences. Our nation's choices and those made throughout the world affect us by affecting morality's direction. The psalmist proclaimed, "Blessed is the nation whose God is the Lord" (Psalm 33:12). Furthermore, God said, "*If* my people, who are called by my name, will humble themselves and pray and seek my face and turn from their wicked ways, then I will hear from Heaven, and I will forgive their sin and will heal their land. Now my eyes will be open and my ears attentive to the prayers offered in this place" (2 Chronicles 7:14, 15; emphasis mine). Praying for the entire world can help in breaking the bondage of abuse gripping the world.

4. Nehemiah meditated on the Lord's faithfulness, strength, and restoration.

Meditate on the Lord's presence and faithfulness in your life. Speak His Word into your weakness, inviting Him into the deepest recesses of your heart and soul. In doing so you will change your spiritual atmosphere. Let God be God. Allow Him to work in ways you never dreamed possible rather than in the limited scope other people may have claimed. The mighty wonders of God recorded in Scripture are evidence of power accessible to you as His child. Let God's Word empower you while embracing the freedom He offers in your relationship with Him. He's your heavenly Father; let Him treat you like His daughter, His princess.

5. Upon receiving confirmation God would be with him, Nehemiah never wavered in his commitment despite his fear.

Nehemiah declared, "I was very much afraid. . . . Then I prayed to the God of Heaven" (2:2, 4). Remember: fear is of the enemy, but God is with you. Move forward.

Terrified at times in my journey of making a new life for myself, I was completely dependent on faith to make the next move. Having no guide except the Spirit within me, there were moments when each step seemed like a blind leap. However, with each step I found myself more empowered for the next one. The point is, I kept moving forward in spite of the voice in my head telling me I was destined for failure. Obviously, my heart needed to be in the right place to hear God's instruction. If I were selfish with impure motives, I would have failed. God knew I was trying to seek His will above all else, and He never let me down, lovingly guiding me each moment and emboldening me when I was afraid.

6. Nehemiah faced opposition.

Nehemiah's opposition included mockery, ridicule, false accusations, lies, deception, intimidation, conspiracy, and even death threats as described in the following passages: 2:19; 3:6-14; 4:1-3; 6:1, 2, 10-13, 17-19. (According to the last passage, Tobiah, an official who attempted to thwart Nehemiah's efforts, believed that because he was from a powerful family, he could intimidate Nehemiah.) However, Nehemiah's response was always one of faith and determination (2:20; 4:4, 5, 13-15; 6:2-9).

As a victim facing these same scenarios, trust that God is working. Don't be afraid.

Having been in the ministry, I faced immense pressure as I started my new life on my own. Adding to the pressure was my husband's attempts to get me back. He manipulated numerous people into texting or emailing me with their concerns about my decision and their overinflated admiration for my husband. I loved these people, but he knew he could turn to them to potentially influence my thinking. During this time I also learned some people believed I left to "sow her wild oats." Though hurtful, their belief didn't deter me. In addition, my husband's "counselor" assured me I would regret my decision not to reconcile. This man used horror stories of other women he dealt with and claimed it was my God-given responsibility to save the marriage. However, assured of God's confirmation, I remained determined to stay the course. My life now is evidence of how God has proven His faithfulness and honored my effort to be faithful to Him.

7. The wall was completed (Nehemiah 6:15).

God will "complete" you despite the rubble your life is in, but the process will take time. The repairer of broken walls, the restorer of what has been stolen, and the redeemer of all you've lost holds mighty plans for you: "'For I know the plans I have for you,' declares the Lord, 'plans to prosper you and not to harm you, plans to give you hope and a future'" (Jeremiah 29:11). God is still constructing my story, and I am constantly amazed at His favor, faithfulness, mercy, and unbounded love.

As you are transformed, dear friend, you will make new and exciting discoveries about yourself. I remember how excited I was when I came to the realization that I love music, gumballs, and cupcakes—meaningless in the grand scheme, but extremely important to me. Having dismissed the little details about myself—what I loved, what I thought, what I felt—I am proud of all God's thumbprints that make me who I am. He is completing my story, transforming ashes into beauty, replacing mourning with joy, and changing despair into praise. Self-discovery is a beautiful experience I wish for all who have lost their identity.

Making the changes necessary for restoration, God will complete your story too, lovely friend, if you respond to His will. Healed on the other side of abuse, you will wonder how God put all the broken pieces back together, and you will be amazed at the process. How you live out the process will make the difference. Check your heart along the way by asking yourself these questions: *Am I glorifying God? Am I trusting Him, or am I still living in fear, shame, and defeat? Am I being faithful? Am I falling more deeply in love with Him as I find freedom and healing? Am I trusting the beautiful, cleansing process of confession? Am I striving to seek God, willing to open my heart to His voice? Am I trusting Him as my Father who wants to shower me with abundance?*

Deciding to leave an abusive relationship can involve extenuating circumstances such as safety issues, children, and insufficient provisions. However, you must take the first step, asking for wisdom from God, the One who provides generously (James 1:5). Although I am not suggesting if or when you should leave, I can offer suggestions so you will not make fear—especially of what other people think—the basis of your decision. Reaching the point where it didn't matter what potentially thousands of people—including my own children—thought about my decision, I knew I needed to make the daunting journey with only my faith in God as my compass. I nearly gave my life to stay in the marriage, and I rested in the fact that God knew this. Seeing what no one else saw and knowing what no one else knew, He had my back; nothing else mattered. Faith was my only resource, and it was enough. In the same way I want you to know God has you, sweet friend. You and God will determine how your journey to freedom and peace will unfold.

Taking Responsibility

As I have come to terms with my past, I have taken responsibility for my part. By sharing what I should have done differently, I hope to help other victims gain insight into their situations:

- Instead of being a victim, I never should have married my ex-husband. However, I would do it again because I have my children and have been able to use my past to help other women.

- I should have exposed my ex-husband to family, friends, the church, and even law enforcement.

- I never should have given my allegiance, nor submitted to or agreed with anything my ex-husband did against my better judgement or my children's mental, emotional, spiritual, and physical well-being.

- I should have protected my children.

- I never should have believed Jesus wanted me to suffer to the extent where I enabled ungodly actions, attitudes, and words. According to 1 Peter 3:17, "For it is better, if it is God's will, to suffer for doing good than for doing evil." Although my actions were based on pure motives, I was extremely misguided in my interpretation of this verse. I did not suffer for doing good. Rather, I enabled evil and suffered for it, and the result did not glorify God.

- I should have realized my value and worth through biblical examples like Deborah, judge of Israel (Judges 4); Priscilla, an evangelist (Acts 18:26); or Anna, a prophetess (Luke 2:36-38.) These women were mighty examples of God's plan for women. I should have studied for myself and not merely accepted what I'd been told about women's roles. More importantly, I should have realized the grace and forgiveness Jesus offered to broken women as exemplified by the woman caught in adultery (John 7:53–8:11) and the woman at the well (John 4:4-26).

- I should have studied what the Bible said about the curse of man's headship over woman (Genesis 3:16) and realized Jesus came to break the curse, which has been twisted by man to control and manipulate women and treat them like property.

- I should have researched the history of men's attitudes toward women during Jesus' time—based on hundreds of man-made religious laws—that considered women evil and worthless except for pro-creation. Jesus' ministry cataclysmically disrupted this mind-set as evidenced in his ministry of teaching women, which was against the law (John 4:4-6), including women among his disciples (unheard of in Jewish culture), and being financially supported by them (Luke 8:1-3). He forgave women their sins (John 8:11). Scripture also reveals a woman first announced His resurrection (John 20:18)—the greatest announcement of all time.

- I should have remembered the message of Revelation 12:10: "I heard a loud voice shouting across the heavens, 'For the accuser of our brothers and sisters has been thrown down to earth—the one who accuses them before our God night and day.'" What Jesus did on the cross silenced the accuser forever. I should not have based my decisions on my fear of accusations.

- I should have known God's grace covered me, His will guided me, His love fulfilled me, His plan provided for me, His arms embraced me, His eyes watched over me, His hand protected me.

I *should* have done so much differently. I *should not* have been a victim.

Moving from the Victim Identity

I am speaking to my broken sisters now: Lovely friend, you are a hero. You wouldn't be standing were it not for overcoming impossible hurdles. As a victor through Jesus Christ, you must not live in shame resulting from your past. Like the stories of biblical heroes exemplifying transformation from failure into victory, ashes into beauty, mourning into joy, you have a story God can use in a mighty way.

Avoid Satan's trap of shame and insecurity. Charles Spurgeon wisely warned, "Beware of no man more than yourself. We carry our own worst enemies inside of us" (*Spurgeon's Gold: New Selections from the Works of C. H. Spurgeon*). When guilt and shame engulf your heart, the tendency is to criticize yourself, to conclude the situation is hopeless. Withdrawing from others, you resort to a negative mentality—exactly what

Satan wants you to do. According to John 10:10, "The thief comes only to steal and kill and destroy." Because Satan is a thief who comes to steal your joy, kill your spirit, and destroy your sense of self-worth, he uses shame and fear to trick you into accepting the mentality of your unworthiness. Engulfed in darkness, you make spiritually dangerous decisions based on a faulty opinion of yourself.

To change a defeatist mentality, you must redefine your life, parameters, and goals. Of course, you must own your mistakes, make amends, ask forgiveness, and do the hard work of overcoming the past and leaving it behind. You must know you can be free as reflected in John 8:36: "When the Son sets you free, you will be free indeed." Reinvent the scope of your world; remain constantly aware of how Jesus offers you a world of abundance in saying, "I have come that they may have life and have it to the full" (John 10:10).

REINVENT THE SCOPE OF YOUR WORLD; REMAIN CONSTANTLY AWARE OF HOW JESUS OFFERS YOU A WORLD OF ABUNDANCE IN SAYING, "I HAVE COME THAT THEY MAY HAVE LIFE AND HAVE IT TO THE FULL."

You must start *speaking* and *believing* what God says about you, realizing your value is defined by what God alone says about you. What we speak, we empower. For this reason, you should declare: "I am a daughter of the King of Heaven." Every saved believer has been transferred into a royal position: "But you are a *chosen* people, a *royal* priesthood, God's *special possession,* that you may declare the praise of Him who called you out of darkness into His wonderful light" (1 Peter 2:9, emphasis mine). Make choices based on the promise that you are an heir to the majesty of Heaven. In the dark times your prayer should be, "Forgive me, Lord, for not acknowledging my royal position as your daughter. You chose me as your special possession, and I resolve to think in no way other than the way you think about me." A co-heir with Jesus, you are royalty, a princess. You hold the keys to the kingdom of Heaven, and all its treasures are yours. Walk like it. Talk like it. Live like it.

The Book of Second Kings (Chapter 6) tells the incredible story of God's prophet Elisha and his servant. With the Arameans at war with Israel, the king of Aram was pursuing Elisha to capture him. Seeing the Aramean army with horses and chariots surrounding the city, Elisha's frightened servant asked, "Oh no, Lord! What shall we do?" Elisha responded: "Don't be afraid. Those who are with us are more than those who are with them." And he prayed, "Open his eyes, Lord, so that he may see." God opened the eyes of the servant who then saw the hills full of horses and chariots of fire surrounding and protecting Elisha. Just as the servant's eyes were opened to victory, I want your eyes to be opened to your victory so that it causes you to live in hope and expectation, destined for a future molded by God. Just open your eyes, sweet friend. The God surrounding Elisha with chariots of fire can only be seen with spiritual vision. Remember: "The One who is in you is greater than the one who is in the world" (1 John 4:4).

Stand tall in your identity in Christ, holding your head high. Know who you are and, more importantly, *whose* you are. My wish for you is found in the Book of Ephesians:

> I pray that the eyes of your heart may be enlightened in order that you may know the hope to which He has called you, the riches of His glorious inheritance in His holy people, and His incomparably great power for us who believe. That power is the same as the mighty strength He exerted when He raised Christ from the dead and seated Him at His right hand in the heavenly realms, far above all rule and authority, power and dominion, and every name that is invoked, not only in the present age but also in the one to come (1:18-21).

The Abuser

"Do not consider his appearance or his height, for I have rejected him. The Lord does not look at the things people look at. People look at the outward appearance, but the Lord looks at the heart" (1 Samuel 16:7).

The Abusive Mind of a Narcissist

When I first left the marriage, someone said to me, "I think your husband must be a narcissist." Having no clue what a narcissist is, I began researching the characteristics. Realizing my husband could have been the poster child for narcissism, I felt validated in knowing there was a term that clearly describes the person to whom I was married.

Looking back, many indicators pointed to my husband's narcissism. He showered me with words of love almost immediately within the first few days of meeting him. Although thrilling for my sixteen-year-old heart, these abrupt proclamations should have been a warning sign: it's often called "love-bombing." When a narcissist says "I love you," it's a smothering kind of controlling statement, one that really means, "I love you for everything you can do for me." The love-bombing continued with the abrupt, urgent way he asked my father (without asking me first) if he could marry me. This came after only seeing me three times—especially abrupt considering about seven months passed since I heard from him before his proposal. Having devalued myself because of his silence, his proposal shocked me. The cycle already in motion, he groomed me with compliments and affection from the moment we met—then silence. Then he proposed—and this was jarring—and the love-bombing started again. He pulled me back into his grip immediately; there was no dating period. Once we were engaged he attempted to get me to move the wedding date up seven months, leaving me only three months to prepare. This also would have forced me to put aside my plans to go to mission school. Even though I abandoned my plans to do international mission work to accept his proposal, I still wanted to attend a six-month biblical studies school to expand my Bible knowledge. Although I didn't agree to his request, it indicated his extreme lack of consideration for my plans.

Another of his narcissistic traits was jealousy of people who received recognition or were successful; he considered those people threatening because he perceived them taking the spotlight away from him. Ironically, he would dote on and praise those people—setting them up as heroes—only to devalue and demean them later. Such was the case with my father, church leaders, friends, and family members, especially if the praise he showered upon them was unreciprocated or if they tried to call him out for his infractions. If so, he was ready for all-out war. He had very little use for the few people who could see through his façades.

When I left the marriage and learned about narcissism, I began thinking about what the Bible says about pride. Realizing the many narcissists in the Bible were portrayed unfavorably, I learned how their lives ended disastrously. For example, after disobeying God and blaming others, King Saul lost his royal position, was plagued by an evil spirit, and eventually died by his own sword (1 Samuel).

Psalm 36:1-3 provides a condensed commentary on narcissists: "I have a message from God in my heart concerning the sinfulness of the wicked: There is no fear of God before their eyes. *In their own eyes, they flatter themselves too much to detect or hate their sin.* The words of their mouths are wicked and deceitful; they fail to act wisely or do good. Even on their beds, they plot evil; they commit themselves to a sinful course and do not reject what is wrong" (emphasis mine).

As the Psalmist noted, narcissists "flatter themselves too much to detect or hate their sin" and lack the conviction necessary to repent. The situation is even more twisted when the narcissist believes he has scriptural reasons for what he says and does. Even if a narcissist recognizes his problem, this mere recognition doesn't change who he is. Being sorry for "incidents" but not experiencing the type of sorrow leading to repentance and godliness, the narcissist hasn't identified the root of the problem; the cycle of abuse, manipulation, coercion, and intimidation then continues. Ruled by a standard of "good equals reward" and "bad equals punishment," he must satisfy the need to be "good" in his own eyes to ease his conscience. The religious narcissist thinks, "I know what I'm doing is wrong, but I'm also doing right. I have crossed my t's and dotted my i's. Therefore, my good outweighs my bad." This ignorance is not godly sorrow but a self-absorbed view of his conscience, not a matter of sincerity but of self-preservation. In the narcissist's mind, any good outweighs any bad—no matter how bad. I had this confirmed by a Christian counselor: making a narcissist aware of his need for repentance is almost impossible. I witnessed this with my abuser. He could show remorse but never admit his need to change *who he was.*

> THIS IGNORANCE IS NOT GODLY SORROW BUT A SELF-ABSORBED VIEW OF HIS CONSCIENCE, NOT A MATTER OF SINCERITY BUT OF SELF-PRESERVATION.

Articulating what it's like to deal with a narcissist is difficult. It is like endlessly running in circles psychologically. With the abuser always asserting he is right and his victim wrong, she doubts her logic and keeps running while hoping for a resolution that never comes. Once when my husband backed his truck into a mailbox, crushing the tailgate, he accusingly asked me, "Did you let me do that on purpose?" Somehow, the tailgate's destruction was *my* fault; it was only one instance of blame-shifting during my marriage. From the perspective of a narcissist, he can't be at fault for anything. As a result, a victim's needs and misgivings must be put aside to ensure peace.

Taking responsibility to stroke the narcissist's ego, the victim must appease at all costs.

The Abuser's Familial Responsibility

The Bible is extremely clear about the responsibility of a man to care for his family's emotional, physical, and spiritual needs. 1 Peter 3:10 advises, "You husbands likewise, live with your wives in an understanding way, as with a weaker vessel, since she is a woman; and grant her honor as a fellow heir of the grace of life, so that your prayers may not be hindered." The Old Testament also provides admonitions to men about leading their families in the way of the Lord and teaching them His precepts: "These commandments that I give you today are to be on your hearts. Impress them on your children. Talk about them when you sit at home and when you walk along the road, when you lie down and when you get up" (Deuteronomy 6:6, 7). And, from Proverbs 14:16, "Whoever fears the Lord has a secure fortress, and for their children it will be a refuge." Therefore men, including ministers, who are abusing their wives and children are foolishly walking through a spiritual minefield. Believing they will go unscathed and yet gambling with their relationship with God, these men are deceiving not only themselves but the church.

Furthermore, just because a couple isn't living together doesn't relieve a man of responsibility for his family's needs. I don't think Jesus is pleased with deadbeat husbands who are shirking their responsibility. According to 1 Timothy 5:8, "But if any man does not provide for his own, and especially for those of his household, he has denied the faith and is worse than an unbeliever." God is saying to these men, "Man up, or you are worse than someone who doesn't believe in me."

The lack of care and concern abusive men have for their families is appalling. Consumed with their own desires, they leave their family's financial responsibility to their wives, the government, the church, or the good graces of people who step in to help after a separation or divorce. Incredibly, many times when women leave abusive relationships, their "Christian" husbands provide them little or no financial help. One woman told me her estranged husband sent her about two hundred dollars in five months. Some women have actually been sued by their husbands over settlement disputes. Caught in litigation concerning assets, these women can barely buy food to feed themselves and their children, and they are paying exorbitant lawyer fees while facing the possibility of losing their home and possessions to their husbands.

Proverbs 22:22, 23 sternly warns against these situations: "Do not exploit the poor because they are poor and do not crush the needy in court, for the Lord will take up their case and will exact life for life." In the midst of His agony on the cross, Jesus was genuinely concerned about provision for His mother. According to the Gospel of John, "Near the cross of Jesus stood his mother. When Jesus saw his mother there, and the disciple whom he loved standing nearby, He said to her, 'Woman, here is your son,' and to the disciple, 'Here is your mother.' From that time on, this disciple took her into his home" (19:25-27). Just as the Son of God left a supreme example of providing for His family, a man should ensure his family's needs are met. Furthermore, family members, friends, church members, and law enforcement must hold men accountable for meeting this requirement.

Forgiveness for the Abuser

Trusting my ex-husband can find healing and wholeness through God with whom nothing is impossible, I want his story to be a redemptive one exemplifying Jesus' transformative power. Praying for transformation, I will rejoice if it comes. My forgiving heart is a necessary part of the redemptive process. As I continue forgiving my abuser and all who are engulfed in this evil, I am convinced liberty does not exist without forgiveness. I must find and maintain Jesus' forgiving spirit; otherwise, I remain a victim. Forgiveness is not about my abuser; it's about me. It doesn't require a response or a word of repentance from him; instead, it requires my submission to God's will. Satan cannot have me or my heart. Therefore, out of a heart of obedience and a desire for complete healing for everyone involved, I forgive.

Being angry and living in unforgiveness are very different attitudes. Although I still become angry occasionally, I do so less frequently, and this indicates the healing process is intact. However, my anger burns against injustice and the enemy's destructive schemes. While the Bible tells me not to sin in my anger, God doesn't expect me to be complacent about behavior that breaks His heart. He does expect me to channel my emotions through Him and replace my anger with love and forgiveness. I have been very deliberate about meeting God's expectation. I must view my transgressor through the eyes of Jesus—the way God views me.

However, the prayer took time. When I first attempted to pray for his blessing, I merely began the prayer but then told God I would be back later. I just couldn't do it.

Because Jesus crushed my bitterness and resentment long ago, I have prayed a blessing over my abuser despite what he did to my sons and me. However, the prayer took time. When I first attempted to pray for his blessing, I merely began the prayer but then told God I would be back later. I just couldn't do it. I could pray a blessing into his life when I thought about what he put me through, but thinking about what he put my sons through was extremely problematic. Eventually, however, I sincerely asked God to bless my ex-husband, and I knew the forgiveness process in my heart was complete. Praying a blessing for someone who has hurt you—or worse, hurt your children—is extremely difficult, but it is an important act of obedience that enables you to experience freedom.

The Church's Responsibility

"But God has put the body together, giving greater honor to the parts that lacked it, so that there should be no division in the body, but that its parts should have equal concern for each other. If one part suffers, every part suffers with it; if one part is honored, every part rejoices with it" (1 Corinthians 12:24-26)

The Church as a Safe Place

My friends, the church family must offer women safety and support as they attempt to become emotionally healthy—whether they leave an abusive marriage or define clear boundaries within it. Just after I left the marriage I made the mistake of visiting a church where we had ministered in the past. Already feeling broken, I was appalled when a church leader abruptly warned, "You know you have to go back to him." Adding insult to injury, he was clueless to what I endured and didn't bother to ask. In fact, those were the only words he spoke to me in the weeks I visited the church. Conversations like this must not continue in the church. Instead, these conversations must be replaced by an open dialogue about available options that ensure the victim's well-being.

While the ideal solution is to save marriages, support must also be extended to those who leave. Unfortunately, instead of the church being a safety net for the abused, it often revictimizes victims who are perceived as instigators of trouble and not taken seriously.

Such revictimization must stop. The abused need friendship, resources, love, validation, and respect.

I know of several cases where abused women have worshipped for many years in churches where the congregation neither offered assistance nor checked on them and their children. In one situation, while help came from friends outside the church and even from strangers, the church was nowhere to be found. What has happened to the concept of the church being the family of God? We as church members must minister to the needs of abused women and their children. When speaking of offering food or shelter to the needy, Jesus said, "If you do it to the least of these, you have done it to me" (Matthew 25:40). More needy than imaginable, these women and their children *are* "the least." The church *must* do better.

For those standing at the chasm between God's perfect will and abusive circumstances, there is hope. The church should offer this hope. Probably occurring in most churches across the world, abuse is rampant, but most churchgoers aren't aware of it. I don't have all the answers; I am not a licensed counselor or an attorney. However, I can provide suggestions for implementing change in the church from the perspective of personal experience.

> MORE NEEDY THAN IMAGINABLE, THESE WOMEN AND THEIR CHILDREN *ARE* "THE LEAST." THE CHURCH *MUST* DO BETTER.

Offering Help

If you have the power to do something about abuse, please do. Even the smallest effort can help. For any individual—minister, friend, loved one—whom a victim might contact, I offer the following advice.

Believe the victim. This is perhaps the most important advice. Beginning to talk about abuse is unimaginably difficult for victims. Most people could not or would not fabricate abuse stories. A person known to be levelheaded and "normal" has no reason to lie about abuse. Further, just because the abuser is a friend or acquaintance whom you could never imagine capable of what the victim claims, believe the victim anyway. Women who have contacted me often say, "No one believes me." Hearing the trauma and fear in these women's voices is heartbreaking. When I first left my husband and mustered the courage to begin revealing to my parents the madness I endured, I trembled so violently I couldn't hold a glass of water. I hyperventilated until I felt I couldn't breathe. Sobbing in agony, I was on the verge of a breakdown. Fortunately, my parents believed me. Otherwise, I might have gone into a downward spiral from which I might never have recovered.

Listen. Listen. Listen. It's incredible how therapeutic it can be to just vocalize what's going on—if a victim can even find the words to articulate what she is feeling. So it is important to actively listen. I believe having someone to listen also helps a victim see more clearly the reality in which she is living. When I started discussing my abuse, I realized the insanity I endured for so long and was finally empowered to admit I was an abuse victim. My relief and realization only came because there were people willing to listen.

Take the victim seriously. While believing and listening to the victim is crucial, some victims reveal their stories to people who still don't realize the dire nature of the circumstances and, therefore, give quick and insufficient responses. Unfortunately, the situation is probably worse than the victim portrays; in some instances, her life could be in danger. A quick response without forethought can actually exacerbate the situation. Furthermore, despite any friendship you may share with the abuser, not taking the victim's claims seriously could endanger her as the abuser attempts to silence her to maintain his control.

In processing what the victim says, you must remember abusers are master manipulators. Charming and captivating, they portray themselves as "good ol' boys" or as the most congenial people imaginable. In public they will give you the shirt off their back; behind closed doors they are too often monsters. When their true colors are exposed they usually become vindictive or defensive to save their image by concocting stories about their victims to taint the victims' reputation and paint themselves in a better light. As I wrote earlier, when I left, people who didn't know the whole story claimed that, because I married so young, I was leaving to "sow my wild oats." Realizing I couldn't be responsible for what people said and thought about me, I allowed the life I was leading to speak for itself. Unfortunately, in more severe cases, the abuser may begin stalking the victim and even devise plans to harm her or threaten her life.

Go with your gut. If you see alarming signs, speak up. It won't be easy, and the victim will probably evade questions, be vague with her answers, or even be offended. It's OK. She may not be ready to hear your input let alone accept it. Share your concerns anyway. It may eventually be her saving lifeline, although it may take years. After I left my marriage, many people told me they often felt something wasn't right but couldn't put a finger on it, or they expressed how they witnessed incidents that were concerning. One couple said, "We always saw your relationship with your husband more like a father-daughter than a husband-wife relationship."

Another friend told me what troubled her when she came to visit us in Louisiana. One night while we were at a restaurant, my husband became irate with me for no reason. When our visitor excused herself to go to the restroom, I followed her, making excuses for my husband's behavior. Recalling the incident, she said later, "I thought, 'She is acting like an abused woman.'" The next day, before she left to return home, my husband handed her some cash to help with her expenses. She later told me, "I felt it was hush money, and I never spent it." These comments illustrate the red flags people may notice. In my life, these people failed to inform me of their observations at the time.

Sympathize. Don't Advise. Do not offer uneducated advice or pressure the victim unless she is in physical danger; instead, confirm you are listening and express concern and love. You don't want to give inappropriate advice when the results could be detrimental. If the victim continues wallowing in the muck of her situation, extend grace, allow her time to process what is happening, and be there for her. Often victims will leave or come to the threshold of leaving many times before they actually do so. Express your concerns without telling the victim what to do.

> DO NOT OFFER UNEDUCATED ADVICE OR PRESSURE THE VICTIM UNLESS SHE IS IN PHYSICAL DANGER; INSTEAD, CONFIRM YOU ARE LISTENING AND EXPRESS CONCERN AND LOVE.

Validate the victim by expressing your feelings about what she has shared. Asking questions is crucial. However, be aware you may trigger an enabling response. In fact, the victim may become offended and even upset. Such reactions are default survival tactics victims use to protect themselves.

Years before I left, someone referred to my marriage as "slavery" because of the way I was treated. At first I was offended and very defensive. However, unable to forget the comment, I ultimately began recognizing that perhaps more was wrong with my marriage than I realized (although I wasn't ready to do anything about it). But if my friend hadn't expressed those feelings, I may not have recognized the severity of my situation.

Don't recommend a counselor unless you know the individual specializes in or has experience dealing with abuse. Many times well-meaning clergy, counselors, and church leaders attempt to save the marriage at any cost. They will offer advice like "Work on yourself, and God will work on him." If the victim is coming for counsel on abuse, she has probably already paid dearly for trying to stay. A "he said, she said" counseling session only leaves the victim full of unfounded guilt and overwhelming despair and, many times, empowers the abuser's level of control.

Never insist the victim stay in the marriage. Never give erroneous advice to "submit more," "forgive more," "love more," "serve more," "suffer more," "give more sex," or "talk sweeter." And never advise the victim to "pray more." While I firmly believe in the power of prayer, the victim has probably prayed innumerable prayers. Telling her to pray more makes her feel she can't do enough and she is a failure. In most circumstances she has probably tried everything possible to make herself better, to be more, and to submit to God. No matter how much she "fixes herself," it will never be enough to improve the situation if the abuser is unwilling to change.

Further, don't insist the victim leave unless she is in imminent danger. But—and this is important—let her know it is

OK if she chooses to do so. Regardless, she must decide on her own without being pressured.

Pray with the victim. Ask the Spirit to intervene and guide and heal her. However, don't use your prayer as an advice line or to provide your opinion.

Follow up by checking on the victim. Once she has divulged her heart to you, her instinct will be to retreat because of fear, shame, and guilt. If you disappear from her life, she will feel betrayed again.

Church Protocol

Each congregation must use its God-given judgment in handling abuse in the church. Galatians 6:10 advises, "Therefore, as we have opportunity, let us do good to all people, especially to those who belong to the family of believers." The following suggestions are for establishing a protocol to address abuse.

Consider what Jesus would say. Explore what Jesus says about dealing with sin in the church:

"If your brother or sister sins, go and point out their fault, just between the two of you. If they listen to you, you have won them over. But if they will not listen, take one or two others along, so that every matter may be established by the testimony of two or three witnesses. If they still refuse to listen, tell it to the church; and if they refuse to listen even to the church, treat them as you would a pagan or a tax collector" (Matthew 18:15-17). You have probably never seen an abuser taken through this process in an effort to restore him. In fact, from what I have heard and seen, the church coddles and empowers abusers—even if unintentionally.

IN FACT, FROM WHAT I HAVE HEARD AND SEEN, THE CHURCH CODDLES AND EMPOWERS ABUSERS—EVEN IF UNINTENTIONALLY.

When reports of abuse are not taken seriously, the abuser is able to continue sinning, often believing there will be no consequences. He still associates with the same people within the church and still experiences affirmation and fellowship with no action taken to address his abusive behavior. Meanwhile, the victim retreats into loneliness and despair, often with no support system. Exposure is one of the greatest weapons to dismantle abusive situations because the abuser knows he is being watched. Unfortunately, with exposure comes the possibility of the victim's endangerment. In such cases, precautions must be taken to ensure the victim's safety. Nevertheless, trusting God means trusting the restoration process He ordained to help the victim and hopefully restore the abuser.

Provide a place to share burdens. Victims need a place to talk, whether a living room, coffee shop, or park. Another option is to develop a faith-based support group for abused women. Rather than bashing abusers, dwelling on the abuse, or hashing out details of abusive situations, this group should instead provide an opportunity for Jesus to offer healing and hope. Too many times recovery groups focus on the negative and the brokenness instead of Jesus' healing, restorative, and redemptive power. Sharing God's Word and prayer time specifically designed for abused women who have lost their identity in Christ is key. This needs to be a life-giving time of positive affirmations, one that allows women to see and speak about themselves the way Jesus does. They should not call themselves *codependents, enablers,* or *victims.* To find true healing and recovery, they should leave those identities behind and realize they are daughters of God and co-heirs with Christ. Chosen. Royalty. Allow them to affirm their God-given qualities.

Provide substitute families and mentors. Many of these women have horrible family dynamics within their homes, and some have no extended family to help them heal. Including these women in family gatherings, holiday celebrations, home Bible studies, outings, and vacations can be vital not only for healing but also avoiding the same abuse cycle in future relationships. They need to know what it's like to be "normal." Providing mentors is also conducive to the healing process—both for the women and any children—and can instill life-changing principles in a wounded heart. I love this verse: "God sets the lonely in families; he leads out the prisoners with singing" (Psalm 68:6).

Provide shelter. Provide a temporary home, a safe and secret place where victims can stay.

Women need safe places to go where they can rest and think about their next steps. Various organizations and women's shelters can provide such havens, but ideally churches also can provide their own resources, including members' vacation homes and hotel rooms paid for by the church. Keep in mind any legal and safety issues must be researched and applied.

Establish liaisons with professionals. Provide services or connections through various organizations and access to counselors (preferably faith-based) specializing in domestic abuse and children's trauma (including sexual abuse); medical professionals; law enforcement professionals willing to come to the aid of abuse victims; and lawyers who can assist with property litigation, restraining orders, and safety protocol (especially those who can work pro bono or at greatly reduced fees). Conversations and informational meetings with these liaisons are necessary to establish a protocol so church leaders know how to proceed.

Establish connections for meeting urgent physical needs. Contact businesses such as grocery stores, restaurants, fast-food chains, drug stores, furniture outlets, and secondhand stores. Many of these are often willing to provide free or reduced-priced items to victims who have just fled or separated. Many times these businesses have budgets for charitable contributions. A phone call or visit may be the only thing needed to establish such a connection.

Offer educational opportunities. Make arrangements with schoolteachers, counselors, and homeschool instructors willing to ensure a child's education is maintained during the separation process. Sometimes children of abuse cannot continue public education during this process because of safety and/or secrecy issues, as well as emotional stress.

Establish connections for employment. Often, church memberships include business owners and managers who can employ women as they emerge from abusive situations. Undoubtedly, most members have connections with someone who might employ these women and/or their older children.

Provide transportation. Many women do not have a vehicle when they flee abuse, creating tremendous stress, and this can be relieved with help. Some people have extra vehicles they can loan for a time. Many churches have vans that can be used for transportation to necessary appointments, school, and more. Church members also can offer to shuttle these women.

May God guide churches in supporting abuse victims. If all churches did their part, think how many victims could be truly helped!

Biblical Commentary on Abuse

A pervasive plague in the church, abuse is often swept under the rug. However, it is clearly addressed in the following verses from God's Word, starting with passages that address the victimizer.

For the Abuser:

Psalm 36:1-3 — "I have a message from God in my heart concerning the sinfulness of the wicked: There is no fear of God before their eyes. In their own eyes, they flatter themselves too much to detect or hate their sin. The words of their mouths are wicked and deceitful; they fail to act wisely or do good. Even on their beds they plot evil; they commit themselves to a sinful course and do not reject what is wrong."

Proverbs 16:28 — "A perverse man stirs up conflict . . . "

Matthew 15:18, 19 — "But the things that come out of the mouth come from the heart, and these make a man 'unclean.' For out of the heart come evil thoughts, murder, adultery, sexual immorality, theft, false testimony, slander."

Ephesians 5:25 — "Husbands, love your wives, just as Christ loved the church and gave himself up for her to make her holy. . . . In this same way, husbands ought to love their wives as their own bodies. He who loves his wife loves himself. After all, no one ever hated their own body, but they feed and care for their body, just as Christ does the church."

Ephesians 6:4 — "Fathers, do not exasperate your children; instead, bring them up in the training and instruction of the Lord."

Colossians 3:19 — "Husbands, love your wives and do not be harsh with them."

Colossians 3:21 — "Fathers, do not embitter your children, or they will become discouraged."

For the Victim:

Proverbs 22:24 — "Do not make friends with a hot-tempered person, do not associate with one easily angered, or you may learn their ways and get yourself ensnared."

Proverbs 27:12 — "The prudent see danger and take refuge, but the simple keep going and pay the penalty."

Proverbs 19:19 — "A hot-tempered man must pay the penalty; rescue them, and you will have to do it again."

For the Church:

Proverbs 24:11, 12 — "Rescue those who are being led away to death; hold back those staggering toward slaughter. If you say, 'But we knew nothing about this,' does not he who weighs the heart perceive it? Does not he who guards your life know it? Will he not repay everyone according to what they have done?"

Proverbs 31:8, 9 — "Speak up for those who cannot speak for themselves, for the rights of all who are destitute. Speak up and judge fairly; defend the rights of the poor and needy."

Isaiah 59:14-16 — "So justice is driven back, and righteousness stands at a distance; truth has stumbled in the streets, honesty cannot enter. Truth is nowhere to be found, and whoever shuns evil becomes prey. The Lord looked and was displeased that there was no justice. He saw that there was no one; he was appalled that there was no one to intervene."

2 Timothy 3:2-5 — "People will be lovers of themselves, lovers of money, boastful, proud, abusive, disobedient to their parents, ungrateful, unholy, without love, unforgiving, slanderous, without self-control, brutal, not lovers of the good, treacherous, rash, conceited, lovers of pleasure rather than lovers of God—having a form of godliness but denying its power. *Have nothing to do with such people*" (emphasis mine).

These are just a few of the verses applying to abuse. Other passages throughout the Bible shed light on the subject, providing valuable insight to anyone faced with abusive situations.

Abuse and Divorce in the Church

In writing this section, seemingly balancing the church on the one hand and marriage on the other, I could sound as if I am attempting to discredit two God-ordained institutions. One wrong word and the scale could tip. My concern is not whether people agree with me, but whether I am correctly handling the biblical interpretation of abusive marriages leading to divorce in light of the view of some church leaders on this subject. Every idea and word must be sanctioned—anointed—by the Holy Spirit. Though I don't claim to be inspired as the apostles were, I believe God has given me insight into the burdensome subject of abuse in Christian relationships through my experience with and research on this subject. Knowing I tread on holy ground, I carefully press onward, aware I shoulder a great responsibility.

Although I do not blame the church for abuse, I have regrettably found that many times those who turn to the church for help are, as noted earlier, revictimized. Although the victimization may be unintentional, I believe it stems from a deplorable lack of knowledge regarding how to offer help, fear the wrong advice will be given, or a zealous determination to save the God-ordained institution of marriage at all costs. Consequently, the solution offered to an abuse victim is minimal at best.

To the reader: Abuse is most likely happening within your close circle of friends, church members, or even perhaps your family. If you are led to do something about it, God bless you. However, lest you're tempted to make a judgmental statement about abuse or divorce, let me encourage you to first consider what you would do if your mother, sister, or daughter came to you with unbelievable stories about her husband. Would you take her seriously, or would you shrug her off? Would you cite a couple of Bible verses to ensure she understands marriage is forever and she must not leave under any circumstances? Or would you look for a new perspective on what you have always thought to be true? When abuse hits home, your perception may change as you search desperately for a redemptive answer. Just remember Jesus came to redeem all of mankind.

Grace Instead of Judgment

A symbol of my heritage, the church is very dear to my heart. However, many times when discerning spiritual matters, the church unfortunately defaults to legalism or is governed by a spirit of religion—a man-made attempt to control what is not understood. Instead of speaking from God's heart when trying to probe the gray areas of another person's plight, religion conjures hasty conclusions, often breeding a faulty system of judgment. I understand this default mode because I spent so many years in it. However, my preconceived notions about absolutes and what was right and wrong looked very different when my family's lives were affected by the tragedy of abuse and my subsequent divorce. Fortunately, Jesus is the redemptive answer for people like me who want to serve God yet are trapped in an impossible situation facing an excruciating choice. Offering hope to the hopeless and redemption to all, Jesus came to replace a system of rules and religion, extending His abundant grace in the most difficult scenarios. This grace wasn't cheap; Jesus paid the ultimate price on the cross for ordinary people to experience extraordinary grace.

Adjusting our perception of how far-reaching God's grace is solidifies how messed up we all are. Everyone travels their own journey, and until someone has walked in the other person's shoes, it's best not to judge. Relieving us from the need to have all the answers, God's grace replaces judgment. My friends, since God is so swift to offer us grace, we as members of the church should be grateful enough to extend the same grace to someone else, allowing the Spirit to discern matters of the heart.

Misconceptions

I believe misconceptions exist in the church about the roles of men and women in Christian marriages and concerning the male and female roles in the church. Unfortunately, these misconceptions tend to increase the likelihood of the occurrence of abuse. The following are some of these mistaken beliefs.

Many churches embrace a skewed view of the roles delegated by God at creation.

Genesis 2:18 says, "The Lord God said, 'It is not good for the man to be alone. I will make a helper suitable for him.'" Through my research of the Hebrew meaning of the word *helper (ezer, Strong's Hebrew Lexicon 5828)*, I found the word *ezer* is used sixteen times in Scripture in reference to God rescuing or mightily coming to the aid of His people. For example, Deuteronomy 33:29 says, "Blessed are you, Israel! Who is like you, a people saved by the Lord? He is your shield and helper and your glorious sword. Your enemies will cower before you, and you will tread on their heights." This use of the word helper depicts a warrior coming to the aid of a person in need—a picture of the helper God created for man.

In addition, it is interesting to note that the Hebrew word *suitable (kenegdov, Strong's Hebrew Lexicon 5048)* in Genesis 2:18 does not portray this helper God created for man as a subservient aide, but rather a counterpart complementary to or equally corresponding to the man. Therefore, the Hebrew meaning of the phrase "a helper suitable for him" conjures a shift in the traditional concept of the dynamics of Christian marriage. This is the case especially in light of other verses where the word *helper (ezer)* is used. I once heard a Christian evangelist compare the relationship between man and woman in marriage to the two wings on a bird; both wings are needed for flight. What a beautiful picture.

The husband is the head of the wife, and the wife must submit no matter what she endures.

I am certain anyone who has been in the church has heard all the "Wives, submit" or "Husband is the head" verses (Ephesians 5:22; 1 Corinthians 11:3; Colossians 3:18).

However, Ephesians 5:21 also commands, "Submit to one another out of reverence for Christ." I haven't heard this verse often when speaking of the relationship between husbands and wives because often men in the church are too busy ensuring women are subservient and dominated by male leadership, thus stripping away everything God has made women to be. Manipulating Scripture to fit an agenda, many men in the church treat women like second-class citizens or diminish their God-given talents, keeping them tethered to extremely limited roles in both the church and home. I believe this mind-set exacerbates abuse—even if inadvertently.

Practicing true biblical headship would decrease the number of abusive relationships and, in turn, the number of divorces in the church. Exemplifying biblical headship by washing feet and loving unconditionally, Jesus led by being a servant—purposefully, gently—ultimately giving His life for His followers.

The marriage must be saved at all costs.

The book of Malachi (2:26) clearly confirms God hates divorce. However, don't for a moment think He does not hate abuse, as indicated in the verses I included in the previous section. Rather than being a marriage problem with an easy fix, abuse is an ingrained heart problem. Unfortunately, many Christian counselors are unequipped to deal with the issue, and the church turns a blind eye. Consequently, the church defaults to saving the marriage without truly seeking the good of both individuals. Rest assured, God is more concerned about the individuals than the institution.

The abuser can't be guilty of the behavior the victim claims.

Abusers are masters of deception and manipulation. Therefore, people around them must be on guard to avoid falling into their trap. Make no mistake, abusers can charm the birds out of trees and are often perceived as the most genuine of individuals—many times going so far as to portray an image of a savior of sorts, available to come to the aid of anyone in need.

The victim's suffering in her abusive relationship is God-ordained.

This erroneous concept makes the victim feel even more of a failure—hopeless and in despair—causing her to develop a self-imposed guilt complex because she wishes for relief from her suffering. An unspoken and false message in some churches is that suffering is inherently good. These churches maintain Christians are called to suffer in marriage and the marriage will be blessed when they suffer enough. I'm unsure what time frame is being implied in this message; I stayed for thirty years and matters only got worse! If God ordained marriage to increase the amount of suffering we endure, who would want any part of it?

> AN UNSPOKEN AND FALSE MESSAGE IN SOME CHURCHES IS THAT SUFFERING IS INHERENTLY GOOD.

Forgiveness means restoration.

While forgiveness can encourage the marriage's restoration, it does not mean restoration will or should occur in every case. According to the Focus Ministries Domestic Violence Training Manual, only about 3 percent of abusers are actually reformed—a staggeringly low percentage. Abusers are often not held accountable for their behavior, and narcissistic tendencies make change nearly impossible. While the best scenario is for forgiveness and then restoration of the relationship, forgiveness is required and restoration is optional, depending on the case. Restoration may not be possible or even advisable.

My Newfound Liberty

"It is for freedom that Christ has set us free" (Galatians 5:1).

Addressing My Misconceptions

The misconceptions about Christian marriage, abuse, and divorce mentioned in the previous section also shaped my thinking. Consequently, I experienced a much-needed "dressing down" when applying them to myself. In the past I erroneously believed I knew the answers to problematic issues in Christian marriage—most of them had been filtered through what men told me to believe about Christian marriage and divorce. Determined when I left my marriage that no man was ever again going to dictate my beliefs about God or His Word, I began soul-searching and questioning some of the concepts I was taught.

> HAVING BEEN SHAPED BY CONTROL, FEAR, AND MANIPULATION THROUGHOUT MY ADULT LIFE, I RECONSTRUCTED MY ENTIRE BELIEF SYSTEM.

Having been shaped by control, fear, and manipulation throughout my adult life, I reconstructed my entire belief system. Being true to myself and maintaining my integrity were crucial, and I was keenly aware God knew my heart. I would rather have died than misapply His Word to my situation just for the sake of appeasing my conscience. Terrified of making the wrong move, I often wept when considering changing some of my beliefs. I begged God not to allow me to falter, misunderstand, or—most importantly—

disobey Him. This process was not without much pain, but the rewards were countless.

In an effort to hear straight from God—not only about marriage, abuse, and divorce, but also about my relationship with Him—I began readjusting my thinking about my interpretation of His Word. Moving to Nashville and living on my own for the first time in my life, I went everywhere and did everything alone—the best possible scenario for me at the time. Jesus became more real to me in those days than ever before. Experiencing a self-discovery process I never imagined possible, I realized I didn't have all the answers, but I trusted He would lead me. In the past, not knowing God as I should, and fearing He was waiting to condemn my every thought and action, I missed the rewards of a fulfilling relationship with Him. Fortunately, my life changed when I realized God wanted to take my hand and guide me, showing me the abundance of life and love His Spirit provides. Having no idea a relationship with Jesus could be so rewarding, so fulfilling, so incredible, I found more power than I ever dreamed possible.

Discerning the Letter of the Law and Divorce

Faced with the grave reality of my situation, I made a deep and terrifying dive into the confusing world of divorce. Knowing God's Word is perfect, I earnestly strove to live up to His standards. At the same time, I wondered: What if I try a new life and fail? Is there hope for people like me?

Sincerely trying to understand divorce biblically, I read numerous books with various perspectives on the subject. Yet I found I was nowhere closer to an answer than when I started. Mere humans doing their best to expound on a difficult subject, the authors of these books gave simplistic answers straight from Scripture and were very confident of their interpretation, no matter how conservative or liberal. Further, these authors didn't address divorce stemming from abuse.

Still looking for answers, I turned to the Bible. I was hoping God would lead me to some nugget of wisdom I hadn't seen before. I was forced into the realization that the Bible is clear on certain general issues and not so clear on others. For instance, the Bible provides instructions on how to run a home, but it doesn't say what home to buy or where to buy it; the Bible tells us how to be financially responsible by working at a job, but doesn't specify which one; the Bible clearly explains how to develop a godly family, but it doesn't say how many children to have. Of course, these are very simple applications. And in the same way, the Bible gives wonderful instructions for a successful marriage when each party is intentional and careful about following God's will, and it even provides an adultery clause (Jesus' words in Matthew 5:31, 32). However, it doesn't say what a wife is to do when a husband beats her, is addicted to pornography, or demeans her to the point of destroying her God-instilled sense of self-worth. In those cases, one must trust the Holy Spirit for guidance.

As I intently and reverently searched for Scriptures addressing abuse, I made an intriguing discovery. Faithful men of God, and even Jesus Christ, made allowances when keeping the letter of the law was impossible or when the greater good was at stake. Let me clarify with the following examples.

In Second Chronicles 29, King Hezekiah came to power as Jerusalem's ruler. With many of his predecessors being extremely evil, Hezekiah intently sought to reform Jerusalem into the nation God intended. According to 2 Chronicles 29:2, "He did right in the eyes of the Lord." He began radically transforming Jerusalem by repairing the Lord's temple, ridding it of all defilements, and consecrating the people through admonition, worship, and prayers. Initiating a revival of the Passover celebration, he invited all of Israel and Judah to the Lord's temple.

According to 2 Chronicles 30:12, "*The hand of God was on the people* to give them unity of mind to carry out what the king and his officials ordered" (emphasis mine).

Knowing the law stated all who celebrated Passover were to purify themselves, I was struck by these verses: "[M]ost of the many people . . . had not purified themselves, yet they ate the Passover, *contrary to what was written.* But Hezekiah prayed for them, saying, 'May the Lord, who is good, *pardon everyone who sets their heart on seeking God*—the Lord, the God of their ancestors—*even if they are not clean according to the rules of the sanctuary.*' And the Lord heard Hezekiah and healed the people*" (30:18-20, again, emphasis mine). According to verse 27: "God heard them, for their prayer reached Heaven, His holy dwelling place" (emphasis mine). This part of Hezekiah's story culminated in Chapter 31:20, 21: "This is what Hezekiah did throughout Judah, *doing what was good and right and faithful before the Lord his God. . . .* He sought his God and worked wholeheartedly. And so he prospered."

I weep as I read this passage. God blessed Hezekiah because he sought and obeyed Him, and God heard, blessed, healed, and consecrated a bunch of unpurified people because they were seeking God—though the letter of the law could not be perfectly executed. Think of the application of divorce in comparison with Hezekiah and the Jews in this passage. In my situation, because I wholeheartedly sought God, and though I found myself in a less than ideal circumstance, God still confirmed His relationship with me by hearing, healing, and prospering me, seemingly in contrast to what is written about divorce.

In another example, Jesus addressed the subject of making allowances. According to Matthew 12:1-12, "At that time Jesus went through the grain fields on the Sabbath. His disciples were hungry and began to pick some heads of grain and eat them. When the Pharisees saw this, they said to him, 'Look! Your disciples are doing what is unlawful on the Sabbath.' He answered, 'Haven't you read what David did when he and his companions were hungry? He entered the house of God, and he and his companions ate the consecrated bread—which was not lawful for them to do, but only for the priests. Or haven't you read in the Law that the priests on Sabbath duty in the temple desecrate the Sabbath and yet are innocent? I tell you that something greater than the temple is here. If you had known what these words mean, "I desire mercy, not sacrifice," you would not have condemned the innocent. For the Son of Man is Lord of the Sabbath.' Going on from that place, He went into their synagogue, and a man with a shriveled hand was there. Looking for a reason to bring charges against Jesus, they asked him, 'Is it lawful to heal on the Sabbath?' He responded, 'If any of you has a sheep and it falls into a pit on the Sabbath, will you not take hold of it and lift it out? How much more valuable is a person than a sheep! Therefore, it is lawful to do good on the Sabbath.'"

Even Jesus in His perfection made allowances for situations when applying the law would have contradicted His divine purpose of coming to earth—situations that would have imposed an improper regulation or a legalistic and unjust burden. Jesus knew man's misapplication of the law only widened the gap between humanity and grace, justice and mercy, sin and atonement. Illustrating the grace available when imperfect humanity collides with perfection, Jesus ignites hope in me, an imperfect sinner. Despite all my efforts, I am divorced, and this reality is in contrast with God's ideal plan. However, hidden in the shadow of the cross, I stand before Him fully restored and righteous as I live in surrender to Him. He fulfilled the letter of the law so I don't have to. Though Satan whispers to me I am guilty and a failure, the Great Redeemer stands between me and the accuser's firing squad, taking the bullet for me, expunging every guilty charge with His blood.

As I explored the previous passages, I began searching for the redemption in my story and in those of other broken people. In discovering God's nature, Jesus' mercy, and the grace of God's mighty plan for saving mankind, I'm freed from a tormented and hopeless existence. This is a freedom I wish for everyone in the grips of Satan's schemes! I want to speak freedom into every broken soul.

Trusting the Holy Spirit for Guidance

Despite what some people believe, God voices His will to us through His Spirit, guiding Christians in determining the details of their lives. The following Scriptures describe God's guidance in the form of His Spirit.

- "But it is a spirit in man. And the breath of God gives them understanding" (Job 32:8).

- "But when he, the Spirit of truth, comes, he will guide you into all the truth. He will not speak on his own; he will speak only what he hears, and he will tell you what is yet to come. He will glorify me because it is from me that he will receive what he will make known to you. All that belongs to the Father is mine. That is why I said the Spirit will receive from me what he will make known to you" (John 16:13-15).

- "In the same way, the Spirit helps us in our weakness. We do not know what we ought to pray for, but the Spirit himself intercedes for us through wordless groans. And he who searches our hearts knows the mind of the Spirit, because the Spirit intercedes for God's people in accordance with the will of God" (Romans 8:26, 27).

- "For who knows a person's thoughts except their own spirit within them? In the same way no one knows the thoughts of God except the Spirit of God. What we have received is not the spirit of the world, but the Spirit who is from God, so that we may understand what God has freely given us. This is what we speak, not in words taught us by human wisdom but in words taught by the Spirit, explaining spiritual realities with Spirit-taught words. The person without the Spirit does not accept the things that come from the Spirit of God but considers them foolishness, and cannot understand them because they are discerned only through the Spirit" (1 Corinthians 2:11-14).

- "If any of you lacks wisdom, he should ask God, who gives generously to all without finding fault" (James 1:5).

Tortured by the thought I might make a mistake in navigating my life after abuse, I worked hard to remain confident that God would lead me. I based this on the Scriptures listed above and a number of others (even if I couldn't find a chapter and verse for every decision). The Holy Spirit guided me in these decisions. Although I should have been even more confident in His guidance, He was extraordinarily clear in providing a path for me. Though I didn't always follow the path perfectly, grace stepped in, covering mistakes and carrying me every step of the way.

GOD SAW ME AS A 19-YEAR-OLD GIRL HUDDLED IN A BUSH REELING IN DESPAIR; HE SAW MY SHAME WHEN I WAS FORCED TO BECOME A SEX OBJECT; AND HE SAW ME CLIMB OUT A WINDOW IN DESPERATION, ONLY TO RETURN WITH STILL MORE RESOLVE TO KEEP TRYING.

Knowing I nearly sacrificed my life to avoid leaving, Jesus gave me a way out; from then on I relied on God's Word, both written and spoken to me by His Spirit. In my attempt to live in this reliance, the war between condemnation and grace still raged in my head. But God's voice was louder than the enemy's. I was determined to live with this knowledge: "God did not send his Son into the world to condemn the world, but to save the world through him" (John 3:17). I refused to believe I stood condemned for a choice I never wanted to make. With His will being violated long before I packed the Suburban, God saw me as a 19-year-old girl huddled in a bush reeling in despair; He saw my shame when I was forced to become a sex object; and He saw me climb out a window in desperation, only to return with still more resolve to keep trying. I trust He saw it all. In doing so, I ultimately concluded it wasn't God's will for my children and me to suffer at my husband's hands. So I left—and I will honestly say it was without clear Scripture to support my decision. But I trusted the direction of who was leading me and found great assurance.

Confident in knowing I have God's favor throughout this journey, I continue to follow the Spirit's direction, assured in knowing God alone must approve my decisions. To this day, I suppose, some people doubt my decisions, and that's OK because I don't have to answer for their doubts. Constantly proving His favor to me, God propels me forward daily in confidence, fulfilling His purpose for my life. Like the Psalmist, I say to the Lord, "I will praise you to all my brothers; I will stand up before the congregation and testify of the wonderful things you have done" (Psalm 22:22).

God's Examination of the Heart

With this newfound confidence in the Spirit's leading, I never wanted to violate God's written Word. I struggled with theological questions: If there was no redemption for me, who nearly gave my life to save my marriage and was forced to walk away from it anyway, how could I proclaim Jesus as the abundant provider of grace and mercy? Did He actually break the curse of sin? Did He really extend grace to the Law's transgressors? I wondered how I could reconcile those issues. I realized that during Jesus' ministry on earth, much of His teaching focused on the heart, not simply on outward transgressions.

As I navigated my new life, I learned divorce is not the unforgiveable sin—though it is against God's perfect will and should be avoided if at all possible. However, there is so much more to divorce after abuse than just sending, receiving, and signing papers—there is a backstory of sin infringing on God's perfect will long before the papers are drawn up. I realized I needed to explore at what point the marriage covenant was broken. The divorce itself did not violate God's will; rather, what caused the divorce was my husband's destructive patterns beginning long before we were married. My husband's toxic heart issues were manifested outwardly, and the poison spilled into all of his relationships—including our marriage—inflicting massive damage from an early point and onward.

Seeking God's will regarding the choice I was forced to make, I discovered Bible verses I hadn't noticed before, and these helped confirm my decision. I was amazed at what I found. First, I realized if divorce is a sinful act, then God sinned against Himself when He gave Israel and Judah a certificate of divorce because of their unfaithful hearts. In the third and fourth chapters of Jeremiah, God discusses Judah's and Israel's unfaithfulness to Him, comparing it to sexual adultery. Though not the actual act of sexual unfaithfulness, instead it was adultery of the heart manifested in worshipping other gods. In Jeremiah 3:8-10, God says, "I gave faithless Israel her certificate of divorce and sent her away because of all her adulteries. Yet I saw that her unfaithful sister Judah had no fear; she also went out and committed adultery. Because Israel's immorality mattered so little to her, she defiled the land and committed adultery with stone and wood. In spite of all this, her unfaithful sister Judah did not return to me with all her heart, but *only in pretense,* declares the Lord" (emphasis mine). Therefore, God divorced himself from the two nations because of their unfaithful hearts.

Jesus also spoke of matters of the heart being weightier than the physical acts described by the Mosaic Law, such as adultery committed in the heart before sexual immorality was committed (Matthew 5:27-30) and murder committed before physical violence occurred (Matthew 5:21, 22). He spoke of immoral, impure, and hateful thoughts being the seeds in the heart from which adultery and murder grow into fruition.

In the same way, when abuse has occurred for years, the abuser's unfaithfulness goes far deeper than the physical act of violence, and the sexual unfaithfulness is deeper than the physical sexual act. For example, my husband indulged in pornography (committing adultery in his heart from the beginning of our marriage); he was unfaithful in his covenant to treat me as Jesus does the church; he was not the emotional, physical, spiritual, and financial provider for my children and me that God commanded him to be as exemplified in Jesus; he often disrespected me (screaming, cursing, inciting fear, and inflicting injury) instead of honoring me in the way God intended; and he proved to be untrustworthy by, numerous times, not being forthcoming about his activities. In short, he was so preoccupied with his legalistic view of God and the "rules of marriage" he never examined his heart—at least not on a level that would cause him to change. At least partially rooted in narcissism, this legalism almost destroyed him and ultimately destroyed our marriage.

To further explain, here are just a few of the many examples of how my husband deceived himself into believing he was the husband God "commanded" him to be:

- He never engaged in sex with another woman. However, he was plagued with a pornography addiction and even included real women in his fantasies as in the case of the "preacher pedophile" incident. He also attempted to include another woman in our marriage—stopping short of sexual involvement.

- He very rarely "lied" in the most legalistic sense. However, his words were cunningly deceitful, giving vague and distorted answers to keep from revealing the whole truth. He was a master at "lying without lying."

- He never "hit me." However, he was physically and mentally abusive with me—pushing, screaming, cursing, grabbing. Seeing those behaviors as just a temporary "fall to sin," he did not perceive himself as an abusive partner.

Therefore, in view of Jesus' teaching on matters of the heart and my understanding of God's Word about spiritual adultery, I began realizing his breaking the covenant through spiritual adultery was part of my marriage for many years. The point was not whether my husband participated in sex with another woman or the fact he didn't hit me. Instead, through other sins he committed, he was unfaithful to the marriage covenant, essentially from the first day.

Finding Hope

When I left my marriage, I didn't miss my husband. Instead, I missed what could have been and what I tried to make my marriage be. Missing the community of the "lengthy marrieds" ministry, I grieved. Deeply sensing the loss of everything I tried to save, I was overwhelmed at first.

Feeling disconnected, displaced, and excluded, I learned to "do" church all over again, though I had spent all my adult life in ministry. The thought of walking into a church building was daunting, as though I was lost in a sea of strangers. Even the smell of the typical church foyer was traumatic! Furthermore, I felt as if I was infected with a communicable disease and should be yelling, "Hey, I'm divorced! Unclean! You might not want to touch me!" Although distorted, those feelings were my reality as I wondered: *Where do I sit? Who do I talk to?* Even passing the collection basket was awkward. When I once sang like a songbird at the top of my lungs, I found myself whispering on the back row, not wanting to be seen or heard. How could I have become such a stranger in a place I spent nearly every Sunday morning, Sunday night, and Wednesday night throughout my life? Strange and unfamiliar, church was formerly the place where everyone knew me. Now no one knew my name or, perhaps, even recognized I was there. I was lost.

Sadly, this is the way most Christian divorcees probably feel—lost, fearful, and so very alone. At church they hear about the marriage retreat intended to enrich their marriages or the women's group studying the book *The Power of a Praying Wife* or a couple celebrating their 50th wedding anniversary—all wonderful experiences. But to victims and divorcees, these events are reminders of what has been stolen from them, and they grieve what should have been because the loss is so sad.

What about them? Where is their retreat? What about their many tearful prayers that didn't have the results they desired? What about the 50th anniversary they will never experience? Because victims are misguided in their thinking, all these things make them feel like failures. They are misfits. They suffer PTSD. They are depressed. They are victims and codependents.

They are hopeless and lost. Indeed, they are all these things—until their pain collides with the healing power of Jesus.

However, there is hope for all victims. They are changed when they encounter the Savior who extended magnificent grace to the woman caught in adultery; who saw into the scarred life of the woman at the well and extended to her the living water of restoration; who whispers, "Come to me all who are weary and burdened." Empowerment comes in realizing there is no past too damaged, no story too broken, no night too dark from which He can't rescue all of us. Understanding fear is of the enemy, who is a liar, we must not waste our lives fretting over what the enemy tried to destroy or we will miss the divine encounter. Healing is there for the asking.

We who have been abused can live victoriously. Having found my true identity in victory, I disdain the evil that destroys lives, purposes, and identities. Intent on being a voice for those women who haven't yet found theirs, I want to empower those who are still afraid and hiding in the shadows. I want my life to resound with hope so all will know the enemy has not won.

Questions

"If any of you lacks wisdom, you should ask God, who gives generously to all without finding fault, and it will be given to you" (James 1:5).

I often receive questions through my blog and social media, at speaking engagements, and in random encounters. The following are some of those questions and my responses.

Why did you stay?

It's a tricky question with many answers. Misguided in thinking God wanted me to stay at any price, I stayed because I thought leaving would dishonor Jesus. I stayed for the thousands of members of my various church families I thought would otherwise be hurt. I stayed to protect the ministry. I stayed because I was afraid. I stayed because I was clueless how sick I was. I stayed because my husband never "hit" me. And because a bruised heart and a crushed spirit aren't as visible as a black eye, I didn't realize I was living in abuse. I stayed because I thought I couldn't leave with a shred of dignity intact—especially in the eyes of the church. I stayed because of my sons, though my reasoning on this count was misguided. In reality, I should have left for my sons' welfare. I stayed because marriage was familiar and all I knew for my adult life. I stayed to please others. I stayed to protect family members from pain and embarrassment. I stayed because I didn't see myself as a victim. I stayed because I didn't know I deserved better.

In short, I stayed because I was brainwashed. A common tactic used by abusers and narcissists, brainwashing consists of a systematic attempt to change a victim's attitudes, beliefs, or perceptions through repetitive psychological stress. As I have described, my husband's tactics included threatening to abuse my sons, alienating me from my family, destroying property and belongings, and leaving a church position without arranging other employment—causing me to fear lack of provision for my children. (For a clear depiction of brainwashing in action, the 1962 version of *The Manchurian Candidate* is an excellent movie choice, as is the 1940 thriller, *Gaslight*.)

What about the children?

My children definitely suffered because I stayed in my marriage for so long. I wish I could go back and make changes regarding my children's treatment, but I was misguided in thinking I was doing God's will. Victims shouldn't believe they are doing their children any favors by staying. Children are perceptive and affected by what they are feeling and witnessing in an abusive environment, and it will drain the life out of them. Because of my poor decisions, both my sons were forced to undergo the difficult process of healing.

When considering leaving an abusive marriage, women often incorrectly assume children need their fathers. Knowing the power of paternal influence, God gave fathers an enormous responsibility, and this is depicted throughout the Bible. Sadly, abused children often become perpetrators themselves. Furthermore, children who have been exposed to an abusive situation for most of their lives will sometimes side with the abuser, and if the victim leaves, they will impose guilt on or reject the *abused parent*. Such responses are the result of being forced to believe the abuser is in the right, and the children are projecting their pain on easy targets.

Therefore, the belief that children always need their fathers is simply not true.

Although both my sons were extremely supportive of my decision to leave, their suffering was evident. John, the most consistently and violently abused, was more affected than Seth. Feeling helpless to intervene after they became adults, I trusted God and tapped into my newfound courage and fierce praying skills. Early one morning I began walking around the perimeter of John's home praying for God's deliverance and protection, reclaiming in the name of Jesus the territory where the enemy gained a stronghold through the trauma John experienced. I thrust my hands in the air as though offering my son to God and proclaimed, "Take my son! I can do nothing else. Take him! Please take care of him!" Willingly surrendering to the reality of John's life being in God's hands, I was then free—a memorable Ebenezer moment for me. I raised my "stone of help" just as Samuel had done for Israel thousands of years ago: "[T]he Philistines drew near to engage Israel in battle. But that day the Lord thundered with loud thunder against the Philistines and threw them into such a panic that they were routed before the Israelites. "Then Samuel took a stone and set it up. . . . He named it Ebenezer, saying, 'Thus far the Lord has helped us'" (1 Samuel 7:10, 12). Like Samuel, I knew God heard my prayer in my Ebenezer moment.

> I THRUST MY HANDS IN THE AIR AS THOUGH OFFERING MY SON TO GOD AND PROCLAIMED, "TAKE MY SON! I CAN DO NOTHING ELSE. TAKE HIM! PLEASE TAKE CARE OF HIM!"

What were the convictions in your heart that allowed you to leave?

When my husband nearly killed us both by chasing me in a vehicle, I saw how far he would go to control me. Realizing I was being destroyed and jeopardizing my relationship with God, I began to understand He did not want me to be mistreated. I also realized He could lead, teach, and protect me with His grace and mercy. I was secure in the knowledge I had given everything to save my hopeless marriage.

I decided it didn't matter what thousands of people—including family members—from across the country might think. Realizing I would make mistakes, I also understood how God knew my heart, and this knowledge empowered me. When I started caring only about what God thought, not what people thought or said, I experienced liberation and hope.

What have you learned?

Struggle is part of my story, but being divorced does not mean I'm damaged goods. I've also learned that although my dysfunctional marriage was neither God's will nor my fault, I was responsible for allowing my husband to control me, which is a form of idolatry. However, God's redemption bears itself throughout my story as it does in all stories involving broken people who get back up after devastating falls. God's glory shines most gloriously in impossible circumstances. Lastly and most importantly, I have learned I am strong, courageous, and victorious.

Triumph

"The conclusion, when all has been heard, is: fear God and keep His commandments, because this applies to every person. For God will bring every act to judgment, everything which is hidden, whether it is good or evil" (Ecclesiastes 12:13, 14).

I remember sitting in a car as an 18-year-old newlywed on a dismal, rainy day, feeling lonely and depressed, faced with a life of turmoil. Watching each raindrop tap the window and trickle down a winding path until it finally disappeared, I yearned to chase each one. Every drop seemed to be impregnated with abundant possibilities as they journeyed to destinations unknown, and I knew the places they touched would somehow awaken with new life. Eager to escape and get lost with them, I hungered for the life-giving healing that saturated every drop. Healing rain.

Decades later, that moment remains one of the most significant of my life. I believe, even then, that God was revealing His healing presence to me—a presence that remained with me through every terrifying moment of despair. That same presence is with me now as I near the end of this book. In light of that, I am able to confirm once again: I am not a victim. When I embraced the healing power of Jesus, my identity changed from victim to victor. Falling softly and sporadically like spring rain drizzling from Heaven, that healing slowly meandered through the parched landscape of my heart, soul, and body. Gradually coming to life as I drank in every gentle drop, I blossomed into a new life of victory. Healing rain.

May it wash over all who are hurting or broken.

Now you know my story. I think of the poetic imagery of the female nightingale singing her most melodious song, eclipsed by darkness and enduring oppressive pain with her heart pressed against a thorn. Like the nightingale, I'm still singing in spite of the piercing pain of my story. Sometimes our greatest achievements in life are bought at the cost of great pain, and if God's purpose is accomplished, there is nothing greater I can wish.

As the dawn has broken into my darkness, I turn my face toward the light. I sing a song of hope that heals my every scar and washes away the pain. God's merciful plan is always inscribed with hope. Jesus the Redeemer extends an invitation to create a beautiful melody out of all our painful stories. A song of deliverance.

Although exhausted from the writing process as I conclude this journey, I am at peace and most grateful for the God-ordained events inspiring me to write this book. I am triumphant.

I will close with an affirmation of my life's purpose.

If I can inspire a glimmer of hope in one woman; if I can empower one woman with the healing power of Jesus; if I can enlighten one woman to reclaim God's incredible, original design for her life; if I can encourage one woman to conquer fear and live victoriously . . . then this book will be a success. And my journey will be worth it all.

From my website: hopeglimmering.com

Jesus, send the rain.